THE AWKWARD SQUAD

THE AWKWARD SQUAD:

REBELS IN ENGLISH CRICKET

JOHN LUCAS

Shoestring Press

Printed by imprintdigital
Upton Pyne, Exeter
www.imprintdigital.net

Typeset by narrator
www.narrator.me.uk
info@narrator.me.uk
033 022 300 39

Published by Shoestring Press
19 Devonshire Avenue, Beeston, Nottingham, NG9 1BS
(0115) 925 1827
www.shoestringpress.co.uk

First published 2015
© Copyright: John Lucas

ISBN 978-1-910323-19-9

ACKNOWLEDGEMENTS

I am grateful to the following who have in different ways assisted in the writing of *The Awkward Squad*: Chris Arnot, Rodney Bickerstaffe, from whom I learned of the existence of the ballad, "Larwood," and who put me in touch with the singer/songwriter, John A. Young of the folk-group, "The Grey Picker," who supplied me with both text and the song itself. On specific matters of fact I have profited from the knowledge of Jamie Haynes, John Langton, Peter Wynne Thomas and Chris Wakefield; from Kit Wright I heard a good story about Roly Jenkins; and I owe a debt of gratitude to Tony Ellis for casting a professional eye over possibly contentious matter and giving me the benefit of his legal advice. My greatest debt is to my old friend, Dr. Basil Haynes, co-author with me of an earlier book, *The Trent Bridge Battery: The Story of the Sporting Gunns*. He has been immensely helpful in researching material for and reading and commenting on early drafts of the present book. *Sine qua non.*

For Rod Cahill

CONTENTS

Preface   1
Chapter 1: Introduction   5
Chapter 2: Umpiring and its Discontents   20
Chapter 3: Bowlers as Rebels   26
Chapter 4: Batsmen as Rebels   32
Chapter 5: Worthy of the Hire   44
Chapter 6: Shamateurism   66
Chapter 7: The Rural Scene   76
Chapter 8: Changing Times   83
Chapter 9: Rebels and Loyalists   96
Chapter 10: Rebels For a Cause   108
Chapter 11: Orders Restored   123
Chapter 12: Spirit of the Age   131
Chapter 13: Craft and its Values   142
Chapter 14: Speaking Out of Turn   160
Chapter 15: The Professional Game   171
Chapter 16: New Directions   188
Last Over   204

Selected Bibliography   209

Preface

The book that follows is not meant to provide accounts of all those cricketers, episodes, and contentious incidents within cricket that can be called rebellious. In the first place, my concern is with English cricket. Other cricket-playing nations have had their rebels, individuals who have tilted against authority, or who have banded together to challenge the governance of cricket. They have also known moments of more widely-shared rebellion against the powers-that-were. I have chosen to say little or nothing about these, not because I think them unimportant, but because to have strayed beyond English cricket would have made the book far longer and more cumbersome than is desirable. That said, some of the rebel acts I write about inevitably involve other cricket-playing nations. These include the Bodyline controversy, the Packer affair, and the "rebel" tours of South Africa. But for the most part, the focus is on cricket in the UK.

The questions of what makes for a rebel and for rebellious activity are bound to be controversial. As the following chapters reveal, one person's rebel can in certain circumstances be another's loyalist. And some acts don't in hindsight seem so much rebellious as scape-grace, even if the joyless brigade who for so long ran affairs at Lord's saw every slight departure from their notion of propriety as a threat to the proper order of things. In the early 1920s, anyone who dared to voice disagreement with MCC pronouncements ran the risk of being denounced as a Bolshevik. In the following decade the Bodyline controversy was famously said by some to have endangered the future of Dominion and Empire. And far lesser infractions might incur the threat of, as it were, leg-irons. Banishment from the game was not unknown.

Most of the incidents which once caused ructions now seem laughably trivial and were soon forgotten or, if remembered at all, are looked on as little more than capers. Others had a more lasting effect. Reading through the history of cricket it's possible to feel that if, as Oscar Wilde said, work is the curse of the drinking classes, cricket has been their blessing. A mixed one, though. More than one career foundered on drink, especially when drink sparked a rebellious instinct into dangerous life. But matters nowadays are not as they were. There may be less drinking. There is certainly more tolerance as well as a greater degree of forgiveness, even if this sometimes gives the impression of having been uttered through clenched teeth. Though England is still a society characterised by deference, the degree of subordination, even servility, that conditioned the lives of Players of old has long gone. Readers of a certain age will recall that it was fashionable in the closing decades of the last century for the gutter press to provide occasional headlines about cricketers whose questionable behaviour, including the ingestion of illegal substances, was thought deserving of exposure. But like all fashions this one soon died away, though not before a now knighted all-rounder was temporarily banned from Test cricket by the egg-and-bacon brigade.

Although the all-rounder in question began his career after the distinction between Gentlemen and Players had been abandoned, it is safe to say that in an earlier age he would have been a Player. And as a Player, he would in all likelihood have been treated far more harshly than was the case in the 1980s; he might even have been thrown out of the game, or at all events denied the continuance of his Test career. From the start of cricket as a competitive sport in the eighteenth-century, Players have always had a harder time of it than Gentlemen. This was inevitable. They were, after all, the Gentlemen's employees. They could be hired and fired as whim dictated. They had to watch their step, and even then, and after long years of blameless service, could find themselves suddenly thrown aside. The Notts and England batsman, Joe Hardstaff, when he finally retired from a first-class career of the utmost distinction, remarked that "nobody on the Notts Committee even shook my hand or said thanks. I just got on my bike and rode off." And his is a story that could no doubt be replicated up and down the country and through the centuries.

Nevertheless, many cricketers found the game in which they were professionally engaged to be worthwhile employment, despite the fact that, as John Arlott noted in a fine essay about which there will be a good deal to say toward the end of the present book, they had to put up with comparatively disadvantageous conditions of service. Professional cricketers were, and perhaps still are, of a romantic nature – for which read non-materialistic. They had to be, because Players could be very badly treated by those who saw themselves as the natural Masters of Men.

It is Players, therefore, who, almost entirely, make up the list of rebels with which *The Awkward Squad* is concerned. This explains why what follows is a chronological narrative. The history of cricket rebels has to be seen as part of a wider social history in which relations between Masters and Men have undergone gradual changes, many if not most of them brought about by acts of rebellion or organised protest.

The list of cricketing rebels isn't a long one. There are several reasons for this. John Arlott once pointed out that cricketers were in the long history of the game prepared to put up with their lot. It did at least provide them with more worthwhile employment than work in a mill or down a mine. As a sociologist of Labour History might put it, there was greater job satisfaction to be found on the cricket field than on the factory floor or underground. Then again, cricketers were, and in some ways still are, either by nature or nurture habituated to a kind of stoic acceptance. Bad weather, bad umpiring decisions, bad wickets, bad food, bad changing conditions, bad pay … So? If you knows of a better hole, then go to it. Besides, for some at least, there was the hope that they might become heroes, even as the cliché goes "household names" of a game which for so long enjoyed immense respect and affection. Why put this at risk?

But though cricketing rebels may be few in number, they come in all shapes and sizes. Some are motivated by principle, others by sheer bloody-mindedness, and still others by a spirit of irreverent deviltry. Some of cricket's rebels are well known. Others are virtually lost to history. The aim of the following pages is to do justice to all kinds.

Chapter 1: Introduction

Cricketing rebels? An oxymoron, surely? Cricket and rebellion go together like fire and ice. All the terms derived from cricket that have entered into the common language emphasise the game's non-rebellious nature. The very phrase "it's not cricket" implies a dodge, a wheeze, something corrupt or, more to the point as far as the present book is concerned, behaviour that goes against the nature of the game, that challenges the laws which govern it, the spirit in which it's played. There are of course cheats. There are those who use the letter rather than the spirit of the law to achieve a result they want. W.G. Grace's famous running out of the Australian Sammy Jones at the Oval in 1882 is a case in point. The Australian captain, W.L. Murdoch, played a ball to square leg, he and Jones ran, the run was completed and Jones "walked out of his ground to pat the wicket... W.G. Grace coolly picked up the ball, walked to the wicket, dislodged the bails, and cried 'How's that?' Thoms, who was the umpire appealed to said 'out', and out Mr. Jones had to go. Mr. Murdoch, on seeing what had occurred, said 'That's very sharp practice, W.G.'; and to this day I think it was." The commentator here is the other umpire, Greenwood, as reported in Malcolm Knox's *Never a Gentlemen's Game,* an informative, not to say eye-opening account of cricket between England and Australia up to 1914, of which there will be more to say later.

Given Grace's pre-eminence in the history of cricket, it is inevitable that his use of sharp practice has been well documented. But such practice, however regrettable, doesn't constitute an act of rebellion. Nor is claiming a catch when you know the ball has hit the ground before it went into your hands, nor are the thousand-and-one other dodges from which those who use them hope to, and often do, prosper. The point about cheating is that you don't want to be discovered doing it. Quite the contrary, in fact. Cricketing cheats pretend to act within the Laws of cricket. Cheats try to cover up.

A rebel is very different. A rebel is open about what he does. A cheat doesn't want to be the object of contumely. For rebels it goes with the territory. Without exposure, that is without acknowledged confrontation with what they choose or feel compelled to rebel against, they couldn't be rebels. Sir John Harrington's couplet about Treason, "Treason doth never prosper, what's the reason?/For if it prosper none dare call it treason," doesn't apply to the rebel. Though rebellion inside cricket often succeeds, in the sense that those who have a cause for which they rebel achieve the outcome for which they were hoping, few of them gain much from their success, though others coming after them may do so.

This makes them sound rather noble. And indeed some cricketing rebels are truly disinterested, doing what they do for sound ethical reasons. An example of this is Tom Cartwright's refusal to accept a place in the touring party chosen to go South Africa in the autumn of 1968, a party from which Basil D'Oliveira had been disgracefully excluded. Other rebels are more self-interested, though even here an enlightened self-interest motivates some who have protested against low wages and poor working conditions. Others were simply drunk. And there are, as everywhere, the swaggerers who believe their own publicity.

There are also those who enjoy escapades. Cricketers who want to thumb their noses at authority are not difficult to find; and given the starchiness of that authority, especially when it is connected to or directed by MCC, cheekiness is not merely a welcome relief, it is likely to be widely applauded. It is licensed clowning. But such clowning has to be contained. Clowns may pretend to rebel but, as in all carnivalesque circumstances, cricketing clowns operate within unacknowledged but definable rules. While they may momentarily turn the world upside down, they always help return it right way up. And of course clowns are Players, not Gentlemen, though when the distinction between the two collapsed, the possibility of clowning became more widespread. Escapades could then be perceived as a substantial threat to order. If even would-be-Gentlemen were in on the act, what discord might not follow.

A notorious example of an escapade seen as a threat to the stability of order is the incident that occurred on England's Australian Tour of 1990-1, when David Gower and John Morris took a twenty-minute flight over the Gold Coast ground where the visitors were playing Queensland. The Management was not amused. In fact, members of the Management Committee outdid each other in their Colonel Blimpishness. At an early-morning meeting the following day Gower and Morris were hauled before

Graham Gooch (captain), Peter Lush (tour manager), Micky Stewart (coach), and Allan Lamb (players' representative). The two flyers (below) were accused of not being committed to the tour. Gooch was particularly insistent on the need for loyalty to the cause, which considering his readiness earlier in the decade to sign up for the unofficial tour of South Africa, in the preparation for which all kinds of subterfuge had been required, was richly hypocritical. The errant pair were each fined £1,000, and John Morris never played again for England.

"One would hate to think it has become a crime to enjoy a cricket tour," Christopher Martin-Jenkins wrote in *The Cricketer*. But under Gooch, whose joyless, boot-faced regime was more than bolstered by the splenetic Lush, enjoyment was difficult if not impossible. As David Frith noted caustically in a piece he wrote for *Wisden Cricketing Monthly*: "The fines should ensure that no England player in future will even dare to look up from his crossword puzzle while a game is in progress."

Sympathy to Gower and John Morris, then. But what they did hardly amounts to an act of rebellion, even if that was how Gooch *et al* chose to see what was to all intents and purposes no more than a prank.

* * *

Which brings us to the question of how best to define a cricketing rebel. According to the Oxford English Dictionary, a rebel is "A person who or thing which resists authority or control; A person who refuses allegiance or obedience to or fights against the established government or ruler." The history of cricket is liberally sprinkled with the names of individuals and, more rarely, groups, who fit one or other of those definitions. It isn't difficult to think of cricketers who could at a pinch be thought of as resistance fighters against authority, whether that is the MCC, or the club they play for, or the captain under whom they play. Nor is it difficult to come up with names of those who, for a variety of reasons, have refused obedience to the established governors of cricket.

Rebels are trouble makers. They may be individualists, motivated by purely selfish concerns. And it goes without saying that this is how all rebels are seen by those in authority. But they can also rebel in the interests of the game. Right-wing historians such as David Horspool like to argue that in the social and political worlds rebellions never really succeed. In his detailed study, *The English Rebel*, the most Horspool is prepared to concede is that "a history of failure is not a history of insignificance. Rebellions reveal the alternative histories contemporaries wanted to fight." Well, that's reassuring.

But Horspool doesn't allow for the more important fact that while rebellions may not be immediately successful, in the long run most of them are. "The luckier [rebels] survived their rebellions", he says, though by no means all did. He's thinking of Hereward the Wake, "defeated and pensioned off to obscurity." Thomas Becket, however, was murdered in his own cathedral, Simon de Montfort was "butchered, dismembered, his head paraded on a spear just as his son arrived on the battlefield", and Wat Tyler and Jack Cade, were "stabbed in the heat of their uprisings." Which is true. But the causes for which all these men died eventually succeeded. Suffragettes went to prison in considerable numbers in Edwardian England, and one, Emily Davison, died for the cause. Parliament voted down their plea for universal suffrage. But in 1921 many women got the vote and some years later all of them did.

As one example of a rebellion that brought about change in the world of cricket we could instance the refusal of George Lohmann, the great Surrey medium-pace bowler, to play for England in the Oval Test of 1886 because, so Harry Pearson says, "the match fee for professionals had remained unchanged for several seasons at ten pounds, while the amateurs' expenses had increased annually. The patrician [Plum] Warner," Pearson adds, "would later claim that Lohmann – whom he praised, somewhat patronisingly, for his good manners and intelligence – had been 'ill-advised' by those around him. … However, two seasons later the match fee for pros was doubled, which suggests that, badly conceived or not, Lohmann's protest had had some effect." (*The Trundlers,* 2013, pp 36-7) .

* * *

No need, however, to over-egg the pudding. "Men have died and worms have eaten them," as the heroine of

As You Like It, Rosalind says, adding sardonically, "but not for love." And not for cricket, either. Nevertheless, cricketing rebels have sometimes had a hard time of it. This book had its inception at the moment I heard Simon Mann on BBC's "Test Match Special" ruminate on a remark of his father's about Tom Graveney. Graveney was a superb batsman, Mann senior apparently said, and a joy to watch, yet for all his graceful skill he played fewer test matches for England than might have been expected. "But I suppose there were a good many top-class batsmen around at that time," Mann suggested, as though that were sufficient explanation for Graveney's repeated omission from England teams in the 1960s.

Graveney, it should be said, played in seventy-nine Test matches, which is rather more than most other Test players of his or earlier generations managed. Nevertheless, he should have played in even more. Mann's comment made clear that he had no knowledge of the fact that Graveney had been appallingly treated by his masters when in 1961 he was replaced as captain of Gloucestershire. Rightly aggrieved by being so brutally pushed out of the captaincy, Graveney refused to play under an amateur imposed on the team by the County Committee.

The new captain, C.T. M. Pugh, born in 1937, was ten years Graveney's junior. He had been educated at Eton, joined Gloucestershire in 1959, retired from first-class cricket three years later, and during his brief career as a "steady opening batsman", at least according to the *Who's Who of Cricketers,* had a career average of 18.56. Steady in this context obviously means worse than mediocre. Still, Pugh's table manners were no doubt impeccable.

Worcestershire were keen to register Graveney to play for them. But there was a rule that Players who wished to

11

move from one county to another must serve what amounted to a sentence of two years out of the game before they could join their new county. The rule was frequently waived, but not in Graveney's case. He had refused to serve under an incompetent amateur. No Gentleman, he. Accordingly he was forced to wait in the wilderness for two years until finally, and grudgingly, the MCC gave him permission to become a Player at New Road. There, he throve, and season after season he finished not merely top of the county's batting averages, but very near the top of the country's.

Yet despite this, he wasn't chosen to play for England. He had offended against the "spirit" of the game by challenging the right of his original county's committee to appoint as captain someone who was plainly not worth a place in the side. Then in the early summer of 1966, Graveney was once again named to play for his country. One of the Selectors was Graveney's own captain at Worcs., Don Kenyon, and I can recall Kenyon, after the visiting West Indians had taken fewer than three days to demolish England at Old Trafford, saying in baffled despair that England seemed to have no batsman who could cope with the likes of Griffiths, Gibbs, and Sobers.

And yet Kenyon played with Graveney week in, week out. How could he have overlooked Graveney, of all men?

But maybe Kenyon knew exactly what he was doing when he made the remark. Had he mentioned Graveney's name on air it's at least possible he would have woken some of the backwoodsmen at Lords who might then have taken it on themselves to prevent Graveney's recall. At that time, the MCC President was G.O. Allen, who had been involved in the Bodyline controversy – representing the Establishment point of view, it should be said; and the secretary, S.C. Griffith, was, like Allen, a firm believer in keeping Players in their place. So Kenyon may have been acting with wily intent when, almost by default, it seemed, Graveney was chosen for the second Test at Lord's. In this, his come-back to international cricket, he scored 96 in his first innings and, by the time the series came to an end, with two centuries, one of 109, the other of 165, he emerged as top of the England batting averages. Indeed, his 76.5 was more than twenty ahead of Colin Milburn, second with 52.66.

Mann's assumption that Graveney played comparatively few innings for England because of the competition for places is, therefore, nonsense. Graveney was a rebel. A quiet one, dignified, determined, but a rebel all the same, and his act of rebellion cost him – and England – dear.

A lesser act of rebellion ended Graveney's England career once and for all. At the Manchester Test Match against the West Indies in 1969, Graveney, having scored what Wisden describes as "75 well-crafted runs," used the rest day, Sunday, to travel down to Luton to play in a Benefit match, where he would be leading out a team against a side captained by the former Australian skipper, Bobby Simpson. Graveney was now forty-two and needing to look to his future. The match had been arranged the previous year and Graveney sought Lord's permission to play in it, supposing he were to be included in the Test team. The answers from S.C. Griffith and Alec Bedser, chairman of the Selectors, were vague. Anyway, Bedser said, he had no idea whether he himself would still be on the selection panel come 1969. Graveney pointed out that as he especially wanted to play in the Benefit match, for appearing in which he had been guaranteed £1000, it might be better not to consider him for the Test match.

Bedser was still in charge when the team for the Manchester Test was announced, and Graveney was included. He understandably assumed that permission therefore had been or anyway would be granted for him to play at Luton on the rest day. But to his consternation, he was informed a few days before the start of the Test match that he would be required to remain in Manchester throughout its duration. Going to Luton was out of the question. By then, of course, many tickets for the Benefit match had been sold. Even so, Graveney did his best to contact the game's organisers in order to ask whether it would be possible for him to cry off. Unfortunately, the man in charge was ill in hospital and Graveney felt he had no alternative but to honour his commitment to the game. So off he went.

He got back to Manchester at midnight on the Sunday, and at breakfast the following morning was informed by Bedser that his transgression would be reported to the MCC Disciplinary Committee. As a result, Graveney was banned from playing for England for three Tests, which effectively put an end to his time as a Test batsman. As he himself said, and with what in the circumstances might be thought commendable restraint, "it was a miserable way" to finish his international career.

But what on earth did Bedser think he was doing in treating a senior professional as though he were no better than a naughty schoolboy? Later in this book there will be occasion to note the anger Bedser himself had expressed in the previous decade at what he saw as the shabby, demeaning treatment of the Players by the MCC management, including favours shown to the Gentlemen that were denied to the Players. Yet here he was, rather like Dickens's locksmith, Gabriel Varden, acting as the willing servant of an unjust system.

It was of course that system which had led to the explosive moment in late summer 1968, when, sitting in Worcestershire's changing room, Graveney heard over the radio the announcement of the touring team for South Africa, from which Basil D'Oliveira had been excluded. All those present agreed that as the news sank in, Graveney, usually the most phlegmatic of characters, became incandescent with rage. Such rage does him honour.

* * *

Not all rebels behave honourably. It's difficult, for instance, to feel much for or against Phil Edmonds' determination to wear a Swatch watch prominently displayed on his bowling wrist as a way of advertising a brand which Lord's had forbidden him to do. Edmonds, a financially shrewd operator who spent much of his time during matches checking on his stocks and shares, wasn't short of a penny. On the other hand, the embargo on wearing the watch was petty-minded. His act of rebellion, which led to him being dropped from the England team, hastened the day when cricketers' gear would be covered in sponsor's logos – a marketing ploy which has put money in the collective cricketing purse. But it doesn't compare with Graveney's refusal to play for Gloucestershire under a captain he knew was no good and had only been appointed in order to retain the out-of-date assumption that an amateur ought always to lead the county team.

Nor does it compare with George Eastham's refusal to play for Newcastle when he knew that Arsenal were keen to sign him. Eastham argued that he was being denied the right of freedom of work where and as he chose, and he eventually won his case against those who were guilty of what in legal jargon was called "restraint of trade." This made it possible for other footballers to take their trade wherever they could, and with the lifting of the maximum wage came the chance to earn decent living.

The Eastham case is worth mentioning in this context because it occurred at a time, the early 1960s, when sportsmen were beginning to assert their right to play on terms that were more to their liking than those they had been accustomed to. And this is the moment when in cricket the distinction between Players and Gentlemen was to be abandoned. Equally important, perhaps, cricketers were also beginning to feel that moving from one county to another ought to be their right and that denying them it was in fact restraint of trade. In the early 1960s, Graveney's example was by an large the exception. It is now the rule. And although cricketers cannot expect to equal the wages that even averagely skilled footballers have grown used to (although those on central contracts do pretty well out of them), the movement from county to county is now taken for granted, and no doubt terms and conditions form part of the contract a player (and his agent?) signs.

* * *

The subtitle to *Uncommon People,* by the great socialist historian, Eric Hobsbawm, is "Resistance, Rebellion, and Jazz." In the preface, Hobsbawm tells us that "This book is almost entirely about the sort of people whose names are usually unknown to anyone except their family and neighbours, and, in modern times, to the offices registering births, marriages, and deaths. Occasionally," he adds, "they are known to the police and to journalists in search of a 'human story'." And now, "In the era of modern media, music and sport have given personal prominence to a few who, in earlier times, would have remained anonymous."

Music and sport. Hobsbawm was a jazz aficionado who during the 1950s wrote a jazz column in the *New Statesman* under the pseudonym of Francis Newton. Frankie Newton was an outstanding jazz trumpeter who was born in 1906 and died in 1954. Hobsbawm presumably took the name for his jazz columns both as a way of paying homage to a musician he admired and because it kept his own identity secret from his academic peers, who might have taken a dim view of his slumming. Hobsbawm was also a passionate follower of Tottenham Hotspur, but football being in those days even more infra dig than jazz probably explains why, although Hobsbawm includes "music and sport" as human activities in which rebels have their place, he makes no mention of sporting rebels. There is plenty on Duke Ellington, but nothing on George Eastham. Constant Lambert is quoted but not Harold Larwood. There are entries for Charlie Parker (the musician, not the Gloucestershire slow left-armer) but none for Bobby Peel, the great Yorkshire left-armer whom Lord Hawke sacked for rebellious behaviour.

Neville Cardus, who was both music critic and cricketing journalist, makes plenty of comparisons between music and cricket, not all of them especially helpful or instructive. Cardus is a man for lush or wistful harmonies. The discords struck by rebels are not for him. Derek Birley makes a good point in *The Willow Wand:*

Some Cricket Myths Explored, when he says that in the way Cardus wrote about cricket he "was apt to confuse style with pedigree … [Moreover], despite all the rhetorical flourishes, he gives the distinct impression he is merely using cricket for his own loftier purposes… He needed to elevate cricket by the high-brow comparisons with the world of art." (Birley, *Aurum Press,* 2004, p 196. Revised edn of the book first published in 1979.)

Given such a need, it is hardly to be expected that Cardus would want to pay much attention to cricket's rebels. Unless, that is, he can condescend to them by finding them quaint or treating them as "characters", in their way unbiddable but essentially loveable. This has been the characteristic stance, and, it might be thought, characteristic vice, of English writers on cricket, especially when they are focussing on English cricket. Other nations produce more difficult customers, but then these are less likely to be true to the spirit of cricket. After all, they didn't invent the game.

The Awkward Squad takes a rather different stance. What follows, while being by no means a comprehensive account of "uncommon people," tries to do them the courtesy of taking them seriously and, in the process, offer an account of English cricket to challenge the cosier assumptions which are still peddled as truths, especially by those whom that fine poet, Gavin Ewart, a keen admirer of cricket, described in "Radio Cricket" as

> Prep School boys with nicknames,
> sitting there in their shorts,
> wearing their little school caps –
> wool stockings up to their knees,
> with elastic garters!

That was published in 1989, in Ewart's *Penultimate Poems,* and apart from later burblings about chocolate cake and references to granny's stick of rhubarb, not much has changed since then.

Chapter 2: Umpiring and its Discontents

A rebellion has to be against something. It can't exist in a vacuum. As far as cricket is concerned, two criteria are pretty well essential for rebels to come into existence. The first concerns the Laws of the game. The second, less essential but certainly of great importance, is the hire and payment of cricketers and, following from that, the creation of competitive matches, especially the County Championship.

The history of Law-making and changing has been well documented by Derek Birley in his comprehensive *Social History of English Cricket*. Without rules to a game there can be no game. As the poet Robert Frost famously remarked – he was thinking of what he saw as the disadvantages of free-verse – if you're playing tennis you need a net. It is equally obvious that as soon as there are rules someone will want to test them to the limit or beyond. Going beyond limits constitutes an infringement. If this is done sufficiently often to suggest that there may be something amiss with the particular rules that are being infringed, the sensible course of action is to change them.

But before you can do that you then need agreement among those who play the game as to who has the authority to make the change. The game has to be administered. Cricket of course doesn't have rules, it has Laws. The word itself seems to have an authority not conferred on mere rules. Laws, it is tempting to say, are for the gentry, rules for the plebs. Birley makes the point that in the first half of the eighteenth-century, when the Laws of cricket were settled "by the 'Cricket Club', who played at the Artillery Ground", it was agreed among the gentlemen present that they "would choose from among them 'two umpires who shall absolutely decide all disputes'."

This seems clear enough. But as Birley then adds, the agreement did little to prevent improper influences, "nor did it remotely imply that noble and gentle patrons left important decisions to their social inferiors." (p 27.) The position of umpires in cricket has always been problematic. Umpires exist to interpret correctly and to put into action the Laws of the game. But they are less like judges than the copper on the beat. Moreover, although the umpire's decision may be final, much can be done by interested parties to influence that decision. Umpires are hardly ever rebels, let alone like a bent copper, but their decisions can nevertheless be rebelled against or challenged by those trying to bend the Law. The present book will have comparatively little to say about this, but it is worth noting that while W.G. Grace may be the most famous disputant among those who have questioned the umpire's decision – "Windy day, umpire" – he is neither the first nor last to do so, as everyone who recalls the famous spat between Mike Gatting and the Pakistani umpire, Shakoor Rana, will know. This occurred at Fasalabad in 1987, and deserves to be mentioned here because it acts as a reminder that for all the lip-service paid to the "Spirit of Cricket", rebellious behaviour directed at – or on very rare occasions by – umpires does seem to be a constant.

A few other disputatious occurrences relating to umpires in modern cricket are worth noting, and it seems as well to get them out of the way now, before turning to the real subject of this book, cricketers themselves. But then cricketers who try to influence an umpire's decision or who protest at what they regard as an official's bias are, it could be said, rebelling against not only the spirit of the game but the Law which states that an umpire's decision shall be final.

A refusal to accept this was the occasion for an almighty row that occurred during the Test Match between England and the touring West Indians at Edgbaston in 1973. The English umpire, Arthur Fagg, was more or less accused by the visitors' captain, Rohan Kanhai, of discriminating against the tourists. At the end of two days of what Fagg perceived as unwarrantable harassment, particularly that which followed his rejection of a confident appeal for LBW against Geoffrey Boycott, he announced that he would withdraw from standing for the remainder of the match unless he received an apology from the West Indies management.

No apology was received and Fagg therefore declined to appear on the third morning, when his place was taken by Alan Oakman. But for one over only. As the second was about to be bowled, Fagg marched out from the pavilion dressed in his umpire's coat and stood for the rest of the game, during which a public announcement from the West Indies' manager insisted that the West Indies "are fully satisfied with Mr. Fagg's umpiring."

Which is more than can be said for the row that years later blew up over the Australian umpire, Darrell Hair. There is a piquancy about this. Following the bad feeling generated between the captains of touring sides and umpires Fagg and, then, Shakoor Rana, and in the light of further complaints from teams who felt that umpires' decision had discriminated against them, the ICC decided to institute a rule of appointing neutral umpires for Test matches. This would surely bring an end to charges of discrimination? Some hopes.

Given his history, it is perhaps surprising that Hair made it onto the panel of international umpires. In 1992 he was involved in a number of contentious LBW decisions against Indian batsmen; then, three years later at Melbourne, he no-balled Murilatharan for throwing. (He would later describe the bowler's action as "diabolical.") Finally, in 2006, on the fourth day of the Oval Test against Pakistan, in a famous episode which explains his presence in the present chapter, Hair accused the Pakistani team of ball tampering. He and his fellow umpire, Billy Doctrove, awarded five penalty points to England and offered them a replacement ball. The Pakistani team having in protest refused to take the field after tea, the umpires waited for half-an-hour, then removed the bails and declared that Pakistan had forfeited the game to England. Hair was subsequently banned by the ICC from standing in international matches.

To some, Hair was a rebel, one with a cause. He was, they said or implied, a man who took a lonely, heroic stand against the otherwise bland acceptance by the authorities of widespread dubious practices. Hair wasn't racist. He merely happened to be hostile to those who infringed the Laws and spirit of the game. In a poll carried out by *The Wisden Cricketer,* Hair was voted Umpire of the Year for 2006. And the Australian captain, Steve Waugh, remarked sententiously that "No-one is bigger than the game. The Laws are there for a reason." A leaked ICC report showed that prior to the blow-up at the Oval, Hair was ranked second-best umpire overall of those on the international panel, and that as far as decision-making went, he was number one.

But to others, of course, Hair was a villain: not so much a rebel as someone who deserved to be outlawed, and he was indeed a racist, or so the imputation ran. Pakistan's Javed Miandad and Arjuna Ranatunga of Sri Lanka were among cricketers from the Asian sub-continent who were happy that Hair was banned from standing in international matches, and they said so. In response, Hair claimed he would sue the ICC and Pakistan on grounds of racial discrimination, though he subsequently dropped the pursuit of his case.

* * *

Less well known than the episodes concerning Fagg, Rana, and Hair, is one involving Billy Ibadulla and Ray Illingworth. Ibadulla, who had been a Warwickshire cricketer for many years, joined the first-class list of umpires after hanging up his boots, and at one point found himself standing in a match where the behaviour of the Yorkshire team, at that time captained by Illingworth, left him, he felt, with no alternative but to send in a report of misconduct to MCC headquarters. Then, as now, team captains at the end of each county game were required to complete before sending to headquarters their own reports on the umpire's performance during the match. Enough poor reports and the umpire might lose his first-class status. The idea was to guarantee the umpire's impartiality as well as his ability. But as Ibadulla pointed out, it virtually ensured the opposite. When he went into the Yorkshire dressing room to warn them of the impending adverse report he intended to file, Illingworth produced the captain's card, not yet completed, and stared at it thoughtfully. The implication was unmissable. Go ahead with your complaint and I'll mark your card in a way you won't at all like. When, in a TV programme recorded some time later, Illingworth was asked about Ibadulla's account of the incident, he claimed to have no memory of it. Well, he wouldn't, would he. You could, perhaps, argue that Illingworth was rebelling against what he saw as an undue show of authority by the umpire. You could just as well argue that he was acting against the spirit of the game and that such a show of rebellion does him no credit.

* * *

One other incident deserves to be noted, if only because it provides a juicily comic version of an umpire's impartiality. Jack Bannister tells the story of how he found himself bowling for Warwickshire against an especially obdurate but unadventurous Glamorgan opener. As he handed Bannister his sweater at the end of yet another maiden over, the umpire, that hardened old Australian pro. Cec Pepper, growled, "hit him on the pad for God's sake and I'll give the bugger out LBW." Shortly after that Bannister was replaced by another bowler, to whom he reported Pepper's promise. The bowler soon got past the batsman's forward defensive prod, hit him on the pad, and made a loud, confident appeal. Pepper shook his head in derisive contempt. "Not out," he said, "and don't believe everything you hear from that bloody fool, Bannister." No rebellion there, then.

Chapter 3: Bowlers as Rebels
General Observations

The LBW Laws are probably the most scrutinised and frequently changed of all the laws of cricket. Close behind them come the Laws relating to bowling. Birley remarks that in the game's earlier days "The background to the prolonged and acrimonious dispute over bowlers' actions was the continued domination of batsmen in the upper reaches of the game. The MCC," he adds, "who made the Laws, were entirely complacent about this, because batting was the enjoyable part of the game and the one most members liked. The club employed bowlers to give the members batting practice: they did not employ batsmen to give them bowling practice." (p 64.)

All true, though against this domination of the early game by batsmen it needs to be said that for a long time they had no leg protection, that pitches could be extremely rough and uneven, some made up largely of gravel, others of tussocky, pock-marked, grass, still others pitched on a slope, and that even underarm bowling could do a good deal of damage to various parts of the body. There is a well-known story of the Kent and England all-rounder,

Alfred Mynn, strapped to the roof of a coach because his body was too huge to fit inside, being taken up to London to receive medical attention to both his legs after they were broken by deliveries he couldn't evade.

By the time of Mynn's injury, the size of wickets had been enlarged, and, although the actual pitches had improved, side- or round-arm bowling had, to the horror of many, become not merely acceptable but widely practised.

Not surprisingly, this new-fangled style of bowling had begun as an act of rebellion. In 1806, John Willes (1778-1852), a Kent farmer, produced his round-arm bowling method at Lord's, and was soon barred because, it seems, of its devastating effect on batsmen, who were quite unable to counter it. The Badminton Library Cricket, first published in 1893, and for long a kind of *vade mecum* of the game, is decidedly sniffy about Willes, probably because one of the authors was the Hon. R.H. Lyttleton, very much a Gentleman cricketer and one liable to regard all bowlers as plebeians. The jazz trumpeter, Humphrey Lyttleton, was a scion of the family, though it was a rather more conventional member, Oliver, who as Dean at Wells Cathedral, could apparently never process up the aisle without wondering whether it would take spin.

But R.H. (1854-1939), who according to the authors of the *Who's Who of Cricketers,* "although not a famous cricketer ... was a noted student and critic of the game," played for I Zingari until 1880, and, as an amateur, was all for the arts of batting. The authors of the Badminton book quote John Nyren, Willes's famous contemporary, as remarking that Willes was guilty of "throwing instead of bowling." Willes is also compared unfavourably to "that excellent man, Christian and cricketer, David Harris," who of course bowled under-arm. Harris inspired a couplet quoted by Steel and Lyttleton:

> This is the perfect Trundler, this is he,
> That every man who bowls should wish to be.

The authors don't appear to know that the couplet is a pastiche of Wordsworth's "Happy Warrior": "Who is the happy Warrior? Who is he/That every man in arms should wish to be?" a poem much favoured by public schools throughout the nineteenth century.

The most that Steel and Lyttelton will grant Willes is that he "had a twist from leg," but this dubious gimmick was countered by Freemantle, who, we are told, "went in front of his wicket and hit Willes," because from this position he could not be given out, the ball having " been pitched at the outside of the stump." The Badminton authors certainly won't allow that Willes' act of rebellion against under-arm achieved much. "Whatever Mr. Willes may have done ... William Lillywhite and Jem Broadridge are practically the parents of modern bowling. When Lillywhite came out, the law was that in bowling the hand must be below the elbow. Following the example of Mr G. Knight, of the MCC., or rather going beyond it, Lillywhite raised the hand *above* the shoulder, though scarcely perceptibly." (*Cricket,* p 21.)

In other words, only after a Gentleman has instituted round-arm bowling is it acceptable for others to follow suit. Knight, according to the *Who's Who of Cricketers,* "was one of the first bowlers to defy the Law by bowling 'round-arm' and wrote strongly in favour of the new style of bowling." As a non-Gentleman, Willes can be more or less written out of the record. Not only was his action questionable, it was derided as having been learnt from watching his sister bowling a hoop, though even more confusingly, in *Old Cricket and Cricketers,* (n.d. but probably 1890; front cover below) the author, H.H. Montgomery D.D., identified on the title page as "Bishop of Tasmania, Formerly Vicar of Kennington, (Late

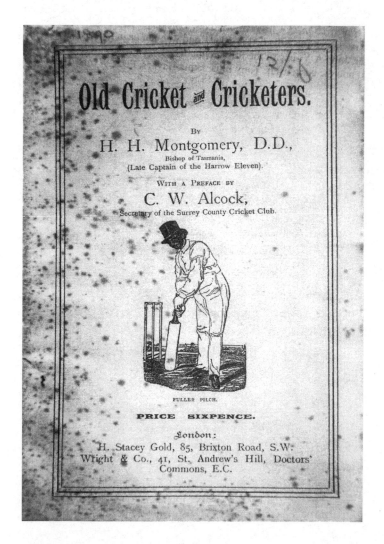

Captain of the Harrow Eleven)", claims that it was "in noticing his sister in delivering the ball turn her hand over" that Willes was inspired to develop his revolutionary method of delivery. (p 68.)

The words of a Doctor of Divinity are not to be taken lightly, though it is difficult to see how or why turning your hand over requires round-arm bowling. You can just as easily perform the action while bowling under-arm. Nevertheless, it seems to be agreed by most early commentators that Willes simply doesn't cut the mustard. According to the *Who's Who of Cricketers,* Willes virtually conspired in erasing his own name from the history of cricket because "in 1822, when playing for Kent v MCC he was no-balled for throwing and was so annoyed by the umpire's ruling that he left the match, vowing that he would never play again."

A rather more charitable interpretation of the incident might conclude that Willes was the first in a long line of bowlers who have been driven from cricket by what was adjudged a faulty action, though in Willes's case the round-arm method he pioneered was soon accepted as permissible. And it has to be said that later commentators, notably Birley, have been far more generous in their appreciation of Willes' act of rebellion.

Nevertheless, from Willes on, bowlers in particular seem to have become identified as rebellious by nature. Though there have been and always will be exceptions, truculent – "defiantly aggressive, obstreperous" – isn't a word you would naturally apply to a batsman, but cricketing journalists often enough pin it to a bowler's name. Truculent, truckle (the grooved wheel that runs smoothly to and fro), trundle. The links are more than sonic. Many bowlers, including the Sussex and England fast bowler, John Snow, came to regard being called truculent as a badge of honour. Not surprisingly, then, Snow's memoir is called *Cricket Rebel: an autobiography,* (1976), and it is no accident that many of the important cricket rebels, or anyway cricketers who regard themselves as rebels, from Sydney Barnes through Harold Larwood to Fred Trueman, have been bowlers. (Though Trueman is a good example of poacher turned gamekeeper.) This leads to a further point.

Given that they frequently found pitches, Laws, and umpires against them, or at all events complained that far too much was tilted in the batsman's favour, and given, too, that many bowlers were treated by captains, spectators and commentators alike as lower order humans or farm animals – carthorses – their rebelliousness isn't to be wondered at. And it can get worse. According to the Oxford English Dictionary the noun "trundle" means, "A small wheel or roller; *esp.* a small sturdy wheel for supporting a heavy weight." Moreover, as a verb, to trundle is "to move or roll on wheels, *esp.* heavily or noisily." The bowler as honest trundler is in other words like a piece of lowly furniture or machinery, to be pushed about, set in motion as and when others dictate. No wonder bowlers wanted to rebel against the imputations contained in the word.

There will be much more to say about bowlers who in the nineteenth century achieved distinction as cricketing rebels, but first I need to say something about batting in cricket's earlier days.

Chapter 4: Batsmen as Rebels

I

There used to be a cricketing commonplace according to which batting was an art and bowling a science. Although calling bowling a science is at least better than identifying it with the kind of passive duty associated with "trundling", the term is nevertheless something of a back-handed compliment. In the popular imagination, scientists are – or anyway were – men (they were always men) who lacked the wit to be artists. They were without creative flair. They were useful but you wouldn't want to keep company with one. Scientists were "stinks", they laboured mole-like in blackened rooms, or they were stained by grease and smoke; and they lacked social grace. Science, after all, wasn't taught at public schools. Nor until modern times did it form part let alone the whole of any degree course at Oxbridge. Science was infra dig. It was for the plebs who, in some circumstances, would later be called "boffins" or, far worse, "geeks."

Scientists were sexually inept. It was artists, those flamboyant creatures, who got the girls. The artist-batsman sauntered to the wicket. The pleb-bowler lumbered up to bowl. Batsmen were debonair. Bowlers had big feet and sweated. Batsmen were aloofly silent. Bowlers uttered a daft, strangulated or belly-deep roar: *Howzat.* No wonder Gentlemen claimed to prefer batting to bowling. Bowling was hard work, it was toil, graft, labour, and it could be unrewarding, too. A batsman who was out cheaply retired to the pavilion, there to sprawl at his ease. A bowler who couldn't get a wicket had nevertheless to stay out in the middle. Or rather, having been taken off, deemed surplus to requirement, he had in open humiliation to loiter at the edge of the field. In the revealing term which signified his abasement, he was "banished" to third man, cow corner, long on.

And yet it would be wrong to conclude from this that in steep contrast to the lonely, workaday bowler, batsmen were always contented members of the cricketing fraternity. As there have been plenty of rebellious artists, so batsmen have been and will continue to be rebellious. Some are born rebellious, some achieve rebelliousness, and some have rebelliousness thrust upon them.

II

Cricket matches in the eighteenth century occasionally ended in acts of crowd violence. These were invariably prompted by events on the field. Consider the following instance, which includes possible cheating by batsmen, by fielders, and, perhaps, by bowlers. To borrow a phrase of Lord Melbourne's, the whole damned caboodle was probably involved. In *The Duke Who Was Cricket*, his biography of the 2nd Duke of Richmond (1701-1752),

John Marshall notes that several of the matches in which the Duke was involved became the subject of controversy. At one a spectator was killed by a stone hurled by rioters. At others, fights broke out over whether one side had played to lose, a matter of great significance when we consider that betting was permitted at any time during matches so closely contested that the outcome might be difficult to call until the very end, at which point one or the other side – or both – could be accused of having thrown or pre-arranged the outcome.

But the example I have in mind is that of the game played in June, 1744, between Kent and All England. It was won by All England, after their "champion," Richard Newland was caught and then, with one wicket left and the odds tilted in favour of Kent, a far easier catch was put down by the "skilled professional Waymark," giving an improbable victory to All England. A sizeable number among the crowd, numbered at two thousand, wasn't prepared to accept either deed. They smelled crooked practice and they said so. Some got into fights among themselves. Others tried to assault the players they accused of cheating.

Were they right? Had Newland got himself out? Did Waymark deliberately drop a catch of which he would normally have made light work? There is no certain answer to either question, nor can there be, but protests abounded. According to which side you were on, Newland deliberately spooned a catch or played an unaccountably daft shot, while Waymark had either accidentally let the ball slip through his fingers or knew exactly what he was doing when he made a mess of the catch that would have won the game for Kent. The phenomenon of "spot fixing", we can infer from the row, was almost certainly being practised on the playing fields of eighteenth-century England, a century when the fate of country houses and a family's fortunes might depend on something as trivial as which raindrop ran fastest down the window of a Gentleman's London Club. Small wonder, then, that those who reckoned they had been witness to dodgy practice rebelled against it. Apart from anything else, many had placed money on the outcome.

Betting on matches or on individual performances seems always to have been a problem for cricket. Marshall points out that in the eighteenth-century, "The true and often fanatical enthusiasts [for cricket] were wealthy landowners who would issue challenges involving high stakes and would build up strong teams from among their employees." (p 40.) Cheating on a large scale was often, and with good reason, suspected. And with this in mind, something must be said of a match which quite puts in the shade the questionable events of June 2, 1744.

What Marshall refers to as a "great cricket match" was played on August 31st, 1731, between "the Duke of Richmond's and Mr Chambers's elevens for two hundred guineas." The match, which was attended by as many as two thousand spectators (meaning, perhaps, "ground full"), ended, as so many matches do, in a draw. Honours even.

Or, it could be, dishonour. For after the result was declared, the Duke's team was, Marshall says, attacked by "irate spectators." He quotes a contemporary account from which we learn that "the Duke of Richmond and his cricket players were greatly insulted by the mob at Richmond, some of them having their shirts torn off their backs; and it was said that a lawsuit would commence about the play." (p 72.)

What caused the near-riot? It appears that after the Duke's team were all out for 79 notches, Mr Chambers's

Eleven had got to within "eight or ten notches" of their target with "four or five" men still to bat, when time was suddenly called. Not surprisingly, those who had bet on Chambers's team coming out on top were convinced they had been cheated of their winnings. And as it was the Duke's men who were subsequently attacked it is not unreasonable to conclude that it must have been the Duke who called time. No surprise then that the game played in 1744 caused such controversy.

These matches are among several whose outcomes raise interesting questions about what constitutes rebellious actions on the cricket field. The behaviour of the Duke's players couldn't by any stretch of the imagination be called rebellious. They knew which side their bread was buttered, and anyway they seem to have batted and bowled to win. And the same holds true of the opposition, or at least of Mr Chambers's Eleven. But even if cheating occurred, the cricketers themselves were presumably following orders. What else, though, could they do? They knew who paid their wages

But the Duke's dodge in calling time – presumably to save him from losing a sizeable wager – caused a rebellion among spectators with good reason to believe that their money had been denied them by a crooked gambit. In which case the Duke of Richmond – the Duke Who Was Cricket – could certainly be said to have rebelled against the spirit of the game.

The incident points to an obvious truth, which is that rebels aren't always models of disinterestedness. Moreover, the rebellious behaviour of those spectators who in August, 1731, reacted violently to what they saw as a trick to bilk them of their winnings is a perfectly good example of vox pop. in action. Social historians have noted that during the

18th century people became increasingly disinclined to put up with what they regarded as unfair laws, all of them enacted for the benefit of the gentry. Enclosure, the taking away of common land, led to severe punishment of poachers, although those found guilty were often doing no more than go where they had always gone. Distrust and indeed dislike of the gentry was widespread, and it seems reasonable to suppose that what happened at Richmond in 1731 points to a wider social issue. It is an example of protest, albeit slight, at the high-handed ways of those who both made the law and thought of themselves as above it, or who thought they could bend it to their own advantage. And even supposing the Duke had behaved entirely properly on both occasions – though he certainly had an unfortunate habit of appearing to act in a suspicious manner – the fact remains that for large numbers of onlookers at cricket matches in which he was involved, he was a cheat. And as he was thought to rebel against the spirit of cricket, so they rebelled against him.

There is no need here to cite other instances of dubious outcomes to cricket matches in the game's early days. *The Awkward Squad* is not intended as a work of exhaustive enquiry and reference. Still, it would be wrong not at least to remark that rebellion and rebelliousness, including that by spectators, go back to the game's roots. Cricket, in other words, has always included examples of that which is not cricket. Moreover, paid cricketers, the Players, can find themselves in an insoluble dilemma. Doing their duty by their captain and/or paymasters may well require employees to rebel against the game's larger considerations. It isn't merely that great bowler, Harold Larwood, who found himself accused of behaving rebelliously because he did as his captain ordered him to do.

* * *

A rather simpler act of rebellion is one which J.L. Carr mentions in his *Dictionary of Extraordinary Cricketers*. In this hugely enjoyable and unverifiable account of individuals who seem as eccentric as was that splendid headmaster, novelist, and cricketer himself, Carr tells us that the cricketing Earl of Winchelsea (1752-1826), president of the Hambledon Club and one of the founding members of the MCC, "withdrew from the 1789 England side because of cold weather." (*Dictionary of Extraordinary Cricketers.)* So much for *nobless oblige*. But then the earl was born with, it might be thought, a licence to rebel.

This was a licence John Snow took on himself when he chose to withdraw from the Oval Test against the West Indies in 1975. According to Snow he was taken ill on the very morning the match was due to start. Such bad luck. According to others, he took one look at the wicket and decided not to bother. Snow wasn't prepared to spend hours of thankless toil against the West Indians in full cry. For that, let Selvey have his swink [work] to him resarved, as Chaucer has one of his cynical pilgrims recommend for St Augustine.

III

As for batsmen who became reluctant rebels in the game's earlier days. A spectacular example of several acting in consort occurred in the summer of 1887, during a match between Notts and Surrey. To understand the ructions this game caused we need to recall that at the time sides were not allowed to declare. Teams were obliged to bat through until all ten wickets fell. But what happened in this match led to a major change. The game's authorities were so taken aback by the outcry following the away side's tactics that two years later a new Law was introduced which allowed for either team to declare an innings closed, although only on the 3rd day. And this Law then stood unamended until as late as 1957, when it was changed so as to permit a declaration at any stage of the game.

Wisden's long and detailed account of the momentous match between the two counties in 1887 begins by telling the reader that "No county match of recent years had been anticipated with greater interest than this, the first meeting of the season between Nottinghamshire and Surrey." According to newspapers and widely-circulated rumours, the greatly-improved Surrey team were thought to be likely challengers for the championship, which Notts currently held. Some eight thousand people turned up to watch the first "bitterly cold and cheerless" day, and despite the comfortless weather the majority went home delighted that the advantage was with Notts. Surrey, batting first, had been bowled out for 115, though even this was something of a come-back considering that at one time six of their wickets had gone down for a mere 27 runs. But as by the close of play Notts had scored 48 with only two wickets lost, everyone thought, and the home supporters certainly took for granted, that their team was in a strong position to win the match.

The next day, however, when the weather was still cold, though not enough to deter "between seven and eight thousand people" from attending, Surrey struck back to such effect that the home team were all out for 89 and, as if that wasn't bad enough, by close of play "Surrey were 183 runs ahead with seven wickets to go down."

Everything therefore depended on what happened on the morning of the final day.

It began well for Surrey – rather too well, in fact. "The 250 went up on the board with only three wickets down, so that the Nottingham men looked forward to an almost certain drawn game." Whether the home side was under orders to bowl negatively isn't clear, but such tactics would have been understandable. And certainly most spectators as well as the players themselves thought it unlikely that all ten Surrey wickets could fall in sufficient time for the home team to try to chase the sizeable total they would be set. The match would therefore potter to an amicable close.

The Surrey captain, however, had other ideas. In the words of *Wisden*, "It was then … That Mr Shuter adopted the tactics which provoked so much discussion in the newspapers. He saw that his side had no possibility of being defeated, while if wickets were thrown away there would be a good chance of winning the match. He therefore gave his men instructions to get out as quickly as possible, and this course they adopted, though in a terribly clumsy fashion. Mr. W.W. Read, who was trying to get his hundred, was caught in the long field when he had made 92 … The last six wickets went down for 25 runs, and the innings was all over for 289."

Notts made a better fight of it in their second innings, but a bad run-out, followed by a dubious LBW decision against William Gunn, handed victory to the visitors, "Surrey winning a remarkable game by 157 runs. The victory was earned by thoroughly good cricket", *Wisden* assured its readers, and "was hailed with great delight by all cricketers in the South of England."

Not, though, in the midlands. Though *Wisden's* report acknowledges the "clumsy fashion" in which Surrey lost their

Surrey

Mr K. J. Key lbw b Attewell	4	– b Shacklock ... 42
R. Abel c Barnes b Attewell	0	– run out ... 44
Mr W. E. Roller b Mee	4	– b Flowers ... 53
Mr W. W. Read b Mee	7	– c Butler b Flowers ... 92
Maurice Read c Daft b Attewell	48	– b Mee ... 28
Mr J. Shuter b Mee	0	– hit wkt b Mee ... 10
G. Lohmann c Sherwin b Attewell	1	– c Attewell b Flowers ... 6
H. Wood c Sherwin b Shacklock	36	– st Sherwin b Mee ... 3
G. Jones c Sherwin b Attewell	5	– hit wkt b Flowers ... 2
J. Beaumont not out	7	– st Sherwin b Flowers ... 4
T. Bowley c Gunn b Flowers	0	– not out ... 0
B 3	3	B 1, l-b 4 ... 5
	115	**289**

Nottinghamshire

W. Scotton b Lohmann	20	– b Lohmann ... 12
A. Shrewsbury c Abel b Bowley	17	– c and b Bowley ... 5
W. Barnes b Bowley	1	– b Lohmann ... 15
W. Gunn c Roller b Bowley	8	– lbw b Lohmann ... 72
W. Flowers b Bowley	6	– b Lohmann ... 3
Mr H. B. Daft b Lohmann	6	– c Abel b Jones ... 12
F. Butler b Lohmann	0	– run out ... 5
W. Attewell b Lohmann	6	– b Beaumont ... 12
F. Shacklock b Lohmann	8	– c sub b Roller ... 1
M. Sherwin run out	12	– c Wood b Lohmann ... 13
R. Mee not out	0	– not out ... 0
B 2, l-b 3	5	B 5, l-b 3 ... 8
	89	**158**

Nottinghamshire Bowling

	Overs	Mdns	Runs	Wkts	Overs	Mdns	Runs	Wkts
Attewell	37	27	36	5	46	29	45	—
Mee	51	27	52	3	25	9	41	3
Shacklock	13	8	17	1	50	26	51	1
Flowers	11.3	6	7	1	41	23	55	5
Barnes					40	15	64	—
Gunn					4	—	8	—
Scotton					7	2	13	—
Mr H. B. Daft					11	6	7	—

Surrey Bowling

	Overs	Mdns	Runs	Wkts	Overs	Mdns	Runs	Wkts
Lohmann	47.2	27	39	5	60	31	66	5
Beaumont	12	10	4	—	22	13	28	1
Bowley	51	41	25	4	36	21	36	1
Mr Roller	6	2	14	—	3	2	1	1
Jones	10	9	2	—	10	6	12	1
Abel					3	1	7	—

Scorecard for Notts v Surrey, May 1896.

last six wickets, it makes no comment on the protests that greeted what was a blatant piece of gamesmanship, whose intent was to get Notts into bat again. A glance at the scorecard reveals that, apart from Read, and Lohmann, who scored one before he was caught off Flowers, the last Surrey batsmen either hit their own wickets or were stumped. What the scorecard *doesn't* reveal is that the two who were stumped deliberately stood out of their ground and the two who hit their wickets did not do so accidentally.

Did the Surrey batsmen rebel against the spirit of cricket? They certainly rebelled against the intention that a side should bat out its innings and defy the opposition to remove them. Acting on their captain's orders, Surrey's lower order chose to remove themselves, and in doing so were either willing or put-upon rebels for a cause – that of achieving victory over Notts. It was this that occasioned the widespread discussion in the national press, one that went on for days, even weeks. Shuter's instructions were either astute tactics or skull-duggery, his team either complicit in or haplessly subservient to his demand that they sacrifice themselves for the cause of victory. What is indisputable was that Surrey had made a mockery of the Law that insisted on a side batting though to the fall of all ten wickets.

A few years later, in 1893 and again in 1896, there was an analogous rebellion, this time directed against the follow-on Law. At that time any side whose first innings score was in deficit by eighty runs or more was obliged to follow-on. In the Oxford-Cambridge matches of those seasons the captains found themselves trying by various tactics, including the bowling of outrageous wides, to out-manoeuvre each other in order to avoid the other team having to follow-on, presumably because they fancied batting again or because their bowlers showed signs of wilting. After much frothing in the press – the *Times* excelled itself in suggesting that this was a crisis of national proportions, which rather puts the matter of Home Rule for Ireland in its place – and much humming-and-hawing at Lord's, the Law was in 1900 amended to permit the captain of the side ahead to choose whether or not to enforce the follow-on. And so matters have remained ever since.

But rebellion was about find a new cause.

Chapter 5: Worthy of the Hire

The increased competitiveness of cricket during the nineteenth century was bound to bring with it increased opportunities and therefore occasions for rebellion. These might be seized by batsmen as well as by bowlers. Wicket-keepers for some reason seem on the whole to have steered clear of rebellious behaviour, though several have been models of eccentricity, and others, among them well-known Test cricketers, by dint of appealing for catches they know they haven't made, or by nudging a bail off and then suggesting that it might have been done by either ball or bat, qualify for membership of the Dodgy Platoon. It is at least possible that two Surrey batsmen were required to hit their own wickets in the contentious match described in the previous chapter because the Notts keeper decided that two stumpings were quite enough and that he wasn't going to conspire any further with the opposition's desire to lose all its wickets.

This may not be sufficiently reprehensible to qualify for enrolment in the Awkward Squad, but during the nineteenth century it can be said that competitive matches were becoming less the prerogative of those wealthy individuals who had dictated much if not most of cricket in the eighteenth century, and far more that of organized clubs, although these were often dependent on Lords Lieutenants and others with money to spare. The County Championship would eventually emerge as the most important such organization. And with its growth, so the opportunity – perhaps inevitability – of rebelliousness increased. And there was a further element which increased the occasion for rebelliousness. This was the rivalry between national sides, or Test Match cricket, as this rivalry became known.

Most of the rebelliousness that goes with Test Cricket belongs to the modern era and will therefore be considered in later chapters of the present book. But one episode, prolonged over several seasons, must be discussed here. It began in 1884 when a touring Australian side, under the captaincy of W.L. "Billy" Murdoch, was asked to take part in a Players v Australians X1 at Sheffield. As was the custom of the day, the County Committee of the ground where the match was to be played chose the team to represent the home country. They also offered a £10 fee to each Player selected for the game. To their consternation, Arthur Shrewsbury, the great Notts batsman, refused to play for what he regarded as a paltry sum, and he persuaded two of his Nottinghamshire colleagues, Billy Barnes (1852-1899) and Wilfred Flowers (1856-1920), to do likewise.

In his *Social history of Cricket*, Birley quotes a newspaper comment that "every well-wisher of the sport will regret the action [the men] have taken." (p 142.) This is not merely unlikely, it is downright silly, given that many of the well-wishers were professional cricketers who were likely to be sympathetic to the cause on which

Arthur Shrewsbury (above) and Alfred Shaw (below).

Shrewsbury took his stand. His act of rebellion not only revealed him to be a champion of fair pay for the professional cricketer, it was the second time he had stood up to Authority. Shrewsbury's refusal to play at Sheffield on the terms offered could and perhaps should have been expected. To explain why, we need to go back a few years.

On Saturday June 4th, 1881, *The Nottingham Journal* carried a long report about unrest at Trent Bridge. Under the headline "Trade Unionism in the Cricket World," the newspaper did its best to offer an impartial account of a very considerable rebellion by players against their paymasters. What had happened was that Shrewsbury and Alfred Shaw, having arranged a match to be played by Notts cricketers against a Yorkshire X1, were sent a letter by the County Committee telling them in no uncertain terms that the game they had planned couldn't take place. To set up such a match was impermissible, and to try to see it through was out of the question. The players were reminded that they were under contract to Notts CCC and that Notts CCC alone was entitled decide which matches its contracted players could and could not play in.

As well as going to Shrewsbury and Shaw, the letter was sent to Messrs Selby, Morley, Flowers, Scotton and Billy Barnes. For a detailed account of what happened next readers are referred *The Trent Bridge Battery: The Story of the Sporting Gunns,* (1985 pp 26-29.) Here, it is enough to note that Shaw and Shrewsbury responded by saying that they proposed to terminate their contracts with Notts, and from now on would act as free agents, prepared to set up and play in matches as and where they pleased. Accordingly, they appeared in no more games that season for Notts.

But the two men were reinstated for 1882, and on markedly improved financial terms from those that had been the part cause of the previous year's rumpus. A sound reason for players arranging their own fixtures was that the money they received from their County Committees simply wasn't very good. As for Notts CCC: the members may not have been bluffing when they sent out their letters, but the loss of such key players had disastrous results not only on the country's cricketing fortunes but on attendances. Hence, the reinstatement of Shrewsbury and his fellow-rebels. The rebels had won.

Shrewsbury, in other words, had form when it came to any assessment of his worth. In his estimation, the County needed him quite as much as he needed the County. So, of course, did English cricket. Nevertheless, there were repercussions from his refusal to take part in the match at Sheffield. In Birley's words, Shrewsbury's recalcitrance "seems to have backfired ... when he went with Shaw and Lillywhite on yet another visit to Australia ... The whole team were this time not only professional, but with the exception of J.M. Read of Surrey, northern." Still, there was trouble. "In one representative match, closely contested, Billy Barnes, a rumbustious fellow from Sutton-in-Ashfield, who was not responsive to authority, particularly when drunk, refused to bowl in either innings when Shrewsbury asked him to." More significantly, Murdoch's team, "had neither forgotten nor forgiven" Shaw and Shrewsbury's refusal to play at Sheffield – a refusal which had inevitably affected the match takings – and were therefore "bitterly hostile" to the visiting team. The tour was, Birley adds, "punctuated by disputes, players' strikes and pained reaction from Australian dignitaries and their press at their 'unpatriotic conduct' which as a result sacrificed 'the cricketing honour of their nation to monetary considerations' and [reduced] cricket to a mere money-making matter." Presumably the Australians were this time guilty of the strikes and unpatriotic conduct, which rather suggests that they had learnt from the English rebels.

Given the limits of the present book, its concentration on English cricket, the Australians' behaviour on this occasion doesn't concern us. Billy Barnes's, however, does. It may not be coincidence that Barnes was born in the same small town as Harold Larwood, and indeed other fast bowlers of marked individuality who at one time or another played for Notts. Hence of course the famous remark about the County recruiting its fast bowlers by "whistling down a pit." Barnes was trouble.

In *A Hundred Years of Trent Bridge*, E.V. Lucas reports Richard Daft as saying that he had unbounded admiration for "Barney." And he records an anecdote of Daft's about how, "on one occasion at Hove … in very hot weather, Barnes, who had made himself a law unto himself, was observed by his captain, Mordecai Sherwin, to be lying down, and was called to order, [and] offered the excuse that he 'could cover more ground that way.'"

In his own *Kings of Cricket*, (n.d) Daft, who hasn't a bad word for anyone, says merely that he thought that as a young man Barnes showed even more promise than either Shrewsbury or William Gunn, and that "there were few batsmen at that time who could equal him. He was for years, I consider, by a long way the finest batsman in England against fast bowling on a hard wicket, his off-hitting and his wrist and elbow play being brilliant in the extreme."

Given that Barnes was also an outstandingly good bowler – "how he could bounce them down", Daft told Lucas – he must have been a hell of a cricketer, and it is odd that *A Hundred Years of Trent Bridge* provides no further comment about him. The reason is probably to be found in Lucas's implicit readiness to offer an emollient account of life at Trent Bridge, an all-holds barred soother. But Billy Barnes was more than being a terrific all-round cricketer.

To understand Barnes in context, some mention must be made of Fred Morley, yet another bowler born in Sutton-in-Ashfield in 1850, who for years opened the bowling with Alfred Shaw. Unlike Barnes, Morley is granted a brief profile in Lucas's book, where he is credited as having reported with wry amusement how, when he and Shaw inspected the pitch before beginning a bowling stint, Shaw would say, "I'm going to bowl at this end, Fred; you can bowl at whichever end you like." Morley was an amenable cricketer. Daft called him a man of "child-like simplicity," although one capable of some wit, as when having failed to enjoy the rough voyage out to Australia with a touring party of 1882, he announced that he planned to make his way home "by the overland route."

Daft's well-meaning words, supported by Lucas's later encomium to Morley, imply that for both of them this is how professional cricketers *ought* to be. Reliable, sober, hard working, uncomplaining. There seems no reason to doubt that Morley was all these things, though when he spoke of taking the overland route home from Australia he was being less humorous than laconic, even tight-lipped. If we are to understand his words aright, we need to look at what "W.G." – this is how the author's name is given – has to say in his *Cricketing Reminiscences & Personal Recollections*. According to Grace, Notts CCC in 1884 were, as so often in the period, the outstanding team and rightly awarded the County Championship, an attainment all the more remarkable for the fact that "Throughout the season they were without the services of Fred. Morley, whose injuries in the collision on his outward voyage to Australia in 1882 kept him out of the cricket-field, and finally led to his death at the close of the season." (p 184.)

Daft says nothing about these injuries, but they were sufficiently severe to bring about poor Morley's death. The matter is set out at some length in *Never a Gentlemen's Game,* by Malcolm Knox. In this detailed, blood-and-thunder, often entertaining account of cricketing relations between England and Australia from the 1870s until 1914, most of them difficult and some decidedly nasty, Knox explains that off Colombo, the *S.S. Peshawar,* the ship on which the visiting party under the captainship of Ivo Bligh was travelling, "smashed into another boat. The liner did not sink, but Morley broke his ribs and damaged his internal organs so severely that he could do little bowling in Australia. Two years later, he would die, supposedly from complications from his injuries." (p 118.) A sad and an untimely death.

But there is more to say. Morley, who was only thirty-three when he died, while being his own man, took good care to keep his individuality within bounds. This is without doubt why Daft speaks so warmly about him. Morley is the very model of a Player. And this is precisely what *can't* be said for his almost exact contemporary, Barnes. Both were sons of Sutton-in-Ashfield, both came from working-class circumstance, both were outstanding cricketers. But there the comparisons end.

Barnes, born in 1852, was nearly fifty when he died, probably because of drink. According to *The Who's Who of Cricketers,* he was the leading professional all-rounder of his day, but on his third tour to Australia – the one to which Birley alludes – "he got involved in a fracas with one of the Australian players and so injured his hand that he missed many of the matches." Knox doesn't comment on this, but then he is kept so busy logging the many fights English touring teams had with Australians – cricketers and the public alike – that he can be excused for omitting mention of the shindig that rendered Barnes *hors de combat.* The account in *Who's Who* concludes by saying that for all Barnes's undeniable brilliance, "He was at loggerheads with the Notts Committee on several occasions and due to this was omitted from the County side two or three years earlier than might otherwise have been the case."

Several occasions? It does suggest that Barnes's unbiddability went beyond the occasional rebelliousness of a professional looking after his own and others' financial interests. According to Peter Wynne-Thomas in his dutiful history of *Nottinghamshire County Cricket Club* (1992), "Barnes was an independent fellow and not one keen on self-discipline… As soon as his form dipped the Committee excluded him from the County side, and a press campaign of 1895 failed to get him reinstated."

In the photograph portrait in *Kings of Cricket* (adjacent, top) Barnes rather glowers, eyes slightly to the left of the camera's focus, not so much wary of it as unprepared to do it the favour of meeting it in a direct gaze. A tall, lean man with a heavy moustache that emphasises the firmly rounded jaw, he does not look as though he is about to do the world any favours. For all that Daft spoke of his admiration for Barnes the cricketer, it seems clear that the all-rounder's determined recalcitrance, his bull-headed refusal to follow his captain's instructions, meant that nobody at Trent Bridge greatly mourned his disappearance from the County team. Whether Barnes is the kind of cricketer who gives rebelliousness a bad name is perhaps

William Barnes in his younger and latter years, respectively.

an open question; but even his warmest admirer would have to admit that he could hardly be thought of as a rebel on behalf of anything or anyone except himself. In rebelling against what they rightly regarded as Notts CCC's high-and-mighty ways and against the taken-for-granted belief that professional cricketers could survive perfectly well on low wages, Shrewsbury and Shaw won victories for other professional cricketers. But Barnes seems never to have been motivated by anything other than what best suited him. He was the rebel as egotist. Others could go hang.

At first blush, Tom Wass (1873-1953), may seem very like Barnes: less a principled rebel than someone for whom the word truculent could have been invented. But this is both to misunderstand and under-estimate him. Yet another Notts right-arm fast bowler of marked individuality, Wass, while not nearly as difficult a man to handle as Billy Barnes, could be intransigent. The photograph of him included in Lucas's *100 Years of Trent Bridge* suggests little of this. In this studio portrait (below)

Wass looks relaxed, square-jawed, the beginnings of a smile on his wide, full lips, and while the eyes gaze steadily out of the picture, the man himself seems the very model of benignity. This is someone you'd be happy to share a few pints with.

But Wass the bowler took no hostages. He was fast-medium to fast, he brought the ball down from a considerable height, he was invariably accurate, he pitched on a length, or just short of it, he proved able and willing to bowl for very long spells, and his total of 1,653 wickets remains a record for Notts. Wass took five wickets in no fewer than 158 innings and was generally agreed to be one of the very best bowlers of the early years of the 20th century, mixing medium-fast leg breaks with the more orthodox fast-medium which was his bread-and-butter style.

Yet despite his generally acknowledged prowess, Wass played in only four representative matches for England. How to explain this? "A plain-spoken man," Peter Wynne-Thomas says, "and someone who would make others aware of his disapproval when necessary, he rather 'frightened' the selectors at Lord's."

In an obituary on Wass quoted by Wynne-Thomas, Pelham Warner remarks that "It is said that the cricket today is somewhat lacking in characters. Wass was certainly one, and, if … he was a 'tough guy' at the start, he mellowed … I do not believe that anyone who played cricket with him will forget him." (*The History of Nottinghamshire CCC.,* p 112.)

Typical Warner equivocation. The fact of the matter is that Wass chose not to bow the knee to those who considered themselves his masters. He went his own way, and if that wasn't the way of MCC, well, so much the worse for them. On one occasion, apparently, he turned up to play accompanied by his sheep dog, of whom he was especially fond. The dog can't stay, he was told. If it goes, so do I, Wass said. The dog stayed.

In his *Book of Cricket* (revised edn 1934, 1947 reprint), Warner provides a brief account of Wass which goes a little further than anything he says in his Obituary. "He was one of the characters of the cricket field. He used to mutter when one stopped a particularly good ball, with a sort of 'How the H– did you play that one' look in his eyes. Once when an umpire decided against an LBW. appeal of his he raised both hands in the air and called on his Maker to witness what an injustice had been done." (p 170.) But this apparently genial account of Wass masks the establishment's disapproval of a great bowler who was sufficiently disrespectful of authority to be classified as Not-One-of-Us. A rebel, in short, though by no means as captious and mulishly disagreeable as Billy Barnes, Tom Wass remained loyal to his County and was wholly admired by a succession of captains. But his refusal to ingratiate himself with the gentlemen of Lord's meant that he played far fewer Test matches for England than his great skills warranted. No surprise, then, to discover that he came from Sutton-in-Ashfield. It must be something in the water.

* * *

The even greater Sydney Barnes (1873-1967), rebelled against the very notion of county cricket. "A rather gaunt, cold character," according to the *Who's Who of Cricketers,* Barnes made two forays into the county game – first for Warwickshire, then Lancashire – but found it "too irksome. Those in authority at Lord's were wary of him ... his name is to be found in only ten Test Matches played in England." Very much the same as Wass. Presumably, the authorities feared that like Wass, Barnes wouldn't take kindly to being ordered about by someone he considered his inferior as, at a guess, he would have taken any amateur captain to be. They had good reason for their fears. For the captains Lord's favoured were invariably batsmen with little understanding or appreciation of the arts of bowling. So, anyway, Barnes seems to have thought. He is sometimes credited with the remark that "When I'm bowling, there's only one captain. Me!" He also said that the one batsman who ever gave him pause was Victor Trumper. "And who else?" he was asked. "No one," Barnes said.

John Arlott, in a piece for *The Cricketer* written for the occasion of Barnes' ninetieth birthday, recalled that the only time he himself saw Barnes bowl the great man was over sixty, but even then he made "the instant impression of majesty, hostility and control." And he adds that "No cricketer who played with or against him has had any doubt that Sydney Barnes was the greatest bowler the world has ever seen." And yet, Arlott continues, after Barnes left Lancashire in 1903 – over a dispute about winter employment – he spent the rest of his career as a professional in League cricket and playing for Staffordshire in the Minor Counties competition. "He was proud of the profession of cricketer," Arlott says, but he "believed, uncompromisingly, that the labourer was worthy of his hire."

It is this which provides the full explanation for Barnes' regular omission from England teams, one that comes straight from the horse's mouth or, you could say, from the Hawke's beak. In his *Recollections and Reminiscences* (1924), Lord Hawke makes only two references to Sydney Barnes, both of them slighting. The first comes when he is gloating over a Yorkshire victory against Lancashire, during which George Hirst "lashed out at Sidney (sic) Barnes as though he was a practice net-bowler." (p 233.) (This, it should be said, is in contradistinction from Arlott's comment that "no-one recalls [Barnes] bowling untidily, nor – amazingly – ever having an 'off day'".)

Hawke's other reference to Barnes comes at the tail-end of his book. Here, Hawke is laying down the law about who should be chosen to play Test Cricket for England. It is, he says, "they who play right through the season six days a week with travelling thrown in. Most unfair would it be to consider for England, at home or on tour, a man from a League who is only occupied with Saturday afternoon cricket – for which, including collections and talent money, he may earn double or even treble as much as a county professional. This was the grounds of my objection at different times in their careers to Sydney Barnes and Cecil Parkin. From those who bear the brunt and toil of first-class cricket should be chosen those rewarded with the few 'plums' that can fall to them."

Hawke deserves credit for introducing winter wages for Yorkshire's professionals – presumably the bone of contention between Barnes and his employers at Lancashire – but it plainly doesn't occur to him that he might done even better by recommending higher wages for all players. Would this have induced Barnes and Parkin to play regular county cricket? Impossible to know, though it can certainly be said that had Barnes in particular done so he would have improved England's bowling no end. Warner claims that "Barnes profited by playing comparatively little cricket, which enabled him to come fresh to each match full of life and energy; but for all that it was a pity he was not more often seen in first-class cricket." (*The Book of Cricket*, p 54.)

But Hawke's refusal to countenance Barnes' being picked for England was as absolute in its way as Grace's rule that "braces will not be worn" by first-class cricketers. Still, at least Hawke manages to spell Barnes's Christian name correctly the second time around.

As for Parkin, (1886-1943), "Cricket's comedian", as he was often dubbed, and, with Wass and Barnes, the other great rebel against kow-towing to the line laid down by Lord's, he did in fact begin his career playing for Yorkshire, but after one match had to switch to Lancashire when it was discovered that he had been born twenty yards over the border. Enough to make a rebel of anyone. As might have been predicted, Parkin, whose fate will be more fully discussed in a later chapter, eventually fell out with and was dismissed by the Lancashire committee, after which he took himself off to see out his career as a League cricketer, although not before playing in ten Test Matches for England.

But if Barnes and Parkin got up Hawke's beak is was as nothing compared with the effect Robert "Bobby" Peel had on him. Neither Barnes nor Parkin were Yorkshire cricketers. Peel was. In his amiable *Twenty Four Years of Cricket* (1912), Arthur Lilley (1866-1929), who played for Warwickshire and kept wicket in 35 Tests for England, spends some time discussing Yorkshire's bowlers during his playing days. He writes warmly of Edward Peate, whom W.L. Murdoch thought was unequalled as a left-hand slow bowler. Then comes the following:

> The mantle of Peate fell upon Peel, a bowler unrivalled
> in his time in his particular style, and also a fine
> batsman and fielder. He retired from Yorkshire's ranks
> while there were still years of good cricket in him. As a

matter of fact, I played with him as a member of an England eleven against the Australians at Truro, some three years after he ceased playing for Yorkshire; but his powers were still apparently unimpaired, in spite of so long an absence from first-class cricket. His bowling retained all its old qualities, and he took seven wickets in one innings, greatly to the admiration of the Australian players, who are no bad judges of the merits of English cricketers.

There is, of course, no question that as an all-round cricketer Peel was far ahead of Peate; for his batting and fielding alone he was worth a position in any team. With his command of length, pace, and break, Peel was a dangerous bowler to meet on any wicket, for he combined excellent judgment with his control of the ball, together with a ready appreciation of a batsman's weaknesses. He was a very sociable fellow, full of good-humour and with a fund of anecdotes. (pp 187-8.)

Peel (1857-1941) sounds from Lilley's account to have been the very model of a model professional cricketer. And in the photograph that accompanies this encomium, Peel is shown in Yorkshire cap, poised to bowl, sideburns and trim moustache reinforcing the suggestion made by his spotless, creased flannels and white boots, of an impeccable professional cricketer. Why then his premature retirement from Yorkshire's ranks?

The answer is that he didn't retire. Lord Hawke sacked him. In his *Dictionary of Extra-Ordinary Cricketers,* J.L. Carr says simply "**Robert Peel,** Yorks. when not himself, was sacked by Lord Hawke for mistaking the pavilion for a batsman and bowling at it." Hawke's *Recollections and Reminiscences* extol Peel's virtues as a cricketer. The author

Robert "Bobby" Peel (above) and Lord Hawke (below).

makes much of the occasion in 1896 when, against Warwickshire, Peel and he put on 292 runs as part of Yorkshire's total of 887. Having praised his own innings – "I do not think I spared a single ball I could score off" – he allows that "the pick of our bunch was certainly Bobby Peel, who carried his bat for 210." (p 143.) A page later he records a victory over Middlesex, in which, "after rain, Peel ran through our opponents, and we were left with 146 to win."

We are next entertained with Hawke's account of how a grateful County presented him with "my portrait and a massive service of plate. It was a more than generous token of appreciation." Hawke was not at first able to express his thanks because "round after round of cheers greeted me." Nor was this all. "Previously I had been the recipient of a gold cigarette-case with the Yorkshire arms and my own in heraldic colours from my own boys. Bobby Peel handed it to me…" (pp 146-7.)

And yet the next year Peel was out on his ear. Hawke is reticent about the cause or causes of this dismissal. He says merely that Yorkshire lost a crucial game to Lancashire which gave Lancashire the Championship, that for the game Peel was dropped, and that, despite this costing Yorkshire the match, it was "an absolutely right decision." (pp 175-6.) The following year, "Wilfred Rhodes came into replace Peel." (p 180.) And that is that.

So what happened? There is no definitive answer to the question, though drink certainly played some part in Peel's sacking. *The Who's Who of Cricketers* says merely that Peel's "County career came to a premature end when Lord Hawke dismissed him for his inebriate habits." Although these "habits" are not fleshed out, stories of Peel when in his cups are legion. He may, as Carr alleges, have once mistaken a pavilion for a batsman and bowled at it, though it seems unlikely. He probably did, as a widely-spread rumour had it, disappear behind the sightscreen to urinate on an occasion when he was taken short. (In another version of the rumour he didn't bother to disappear.) But he must have done something extra special to be sacked. A man who scores 210 not out, who can run through batting sides, and who at a ceremonial event is chosen to hand his captain an embossed gold cigarette-case, is surely entitled to think his tenure as a county cricketer at Yorkshire is pretty secure.

Perhaps that was the problem. Peel may have thought himself entitled to challenge some decision of Hawke's, was marked down for insubordination – in plain terms for being a rebel – and was booted out when, under the influence, he voiced criticism of the noble Lord. A man so sublimely conceited as Hawke wouldn't take kindly to any less than entirely flattering assessment of his own worth. And for a Player at that – unthinkable.

It is inevitable that we compare Peel with another Yorkshire slow-left hand bowler of a later era, John Henry "Johnny" Wardle, although consideration of Wardle's career and its sad end will have to wait until a later chapter. But in both cases it has at least to be said that potentially great careers were brought to premature ends by behaviour that was regarded, rightly or wrongly, as not merely intransigent but as amounting to indefensible rebellion against authority.

* * *

One other bowler needs to be mentioned in this consideration of those cricketers who pre-1914 fell foul of authority. The *Who's Who of Cricketers* has an entry for

Robert Joseph (1864-1940), in which we are told that he played for Yorkshire, "Lower order left-hand batsman, very fast right-arm bowler, *Team,* Yorkshire... His bowling action was very suspect, which probably limited his appearances in first-class cricket." Hawke does not mention Joseph, despite the fact that on one occasion at least the man did England some service. In 1880 the touring Australians, who were running riot over home-based opposition, played a match at Scarborough. According to Malcolm Knox, "Near the end of Australia's first innings, Scarborough put on a bowler named Joseph Frank. (sic.) His eight overs convinced the Australians that he was a 'shier'. Spofforth asked the local umpire if he would no-ball him if he bowled like Frank. The umpire said, 'Yes, you try it.' When Spofforth retorted, 'Why wasn't Frank no-balled?' the umpire answered: 'that's my business.'"

In the Australians' second innings Frank, or Joseph, did considerable damage to various batsman, which culminated in the breaking of the middle finger of Spofforth's right hand. As a result "The Demon" was unable to bowl in the important Test Match at the Oval, which England duly won. Reporting on the tour, the Australian Harry Boyle says of the incident at Scarborough and its aftermath, "We suffered our first defeat at last, after playing 26 matches without losing one. Many old cricketers on the ground said Frank did not bowl fair, and the umpire cautioned him, but would not "no ball" him. Spofforth was not the only one who met with an accident, many of the others being injured." (*Never a Gentlemen's Game,* p 74.)

Joseph isn't perhaps to be accused of having deliberately rebelled against the Laws of the game, but from the sound of it he must have been in breach of them as, getting on for a century earlier, Willes had been. Joseph's is therefore a marginal case. Not a cheat, but, under Hawke, never able to command a place in the Yorkshire team, Joseph may be considered as someone who was never given the chance to rebel against the Laws of first-class cricket. Nor was he deemed worthy of his hire. At all events, he was never, so it seems, on Yorkshire's pay roll.

Chapter 6: Shamateurism

Concern with what was widely called "Shamateurism" in English cricket becomes increasingly vocal during the 20th century. On one occasion it even provoked the normally taciturn Jim Laker into a kind of eloquence. There will be more to say about this later, but the incident deserves to be mentioned here because it typifies an issue that long bedevilled cricket. On the England tour of Australia, 1954-5, Laker's captain, Peter May, having won a £500 bet against an Australian newspaper by scoring a century between lunch and tea, announced that he was turning himself into a Limited Company. When he learnt of this, Laker reflected that he might well have done financially better for himself had he chosen to renounce his professional status. "Amateurs", as he pointed out, were free to take money denied to the Players. who were tied by contract to their employers. Moreover, Gentlemen received tax-relief on all their expenses, which the professionals were denied. Laker's grouse is both understandable and points to a shameless hypocrisy within the post-war game. Gentlemen not only profited from generous expenses, it was by no means uncommon for their Counties to find them salaried sinecures.

But then that had been the case almost from the inception of the County Championship. Before then, as has been noted, cricket teams were funded by rich patrons, who provided both wages and, often, payment in kind – employment and a roof over the heads of cricketers and their families. But once teams began to form themselves into County sides, a variety of devices for filling the purses of amateurs in order to keep them playing cricket for county and, on occasions, country, became common. Back-handers, private arrangements, "considerations", and generous expenses were by no means twentieth-century phenomena, though they became increasingly resented, especially post-1945.

But "Shamateurism" goes back to earlier days of cricket. It wasn't always part of the game. It couldn't be. In both the eighteenth and early nineteenth centuries cricketers tended to be paid in an *ad hoc* fashion. To repeat, those who were hired to play for Dukes and Gentlemen were often also in their permanent employment as gardeners, agricultural workers, labourers of various kinds. Players might be recruited for a season, for a single game, or for a series of matches, and how much and by what means they were paid was a matter between them and their employers. None of these players could be called "shamateurs" simply because there was no pretence that gentlemen were offering their cricketing services for free. There might be – there was – a good deal of dodgy dealing in order to win bets, but as far as is known none of it involved trying to pass off paid players as amateurs or vice versa. Such considerations didn't apply.

But as County Cricket developed, so playing arrangements and the composition of teams inevitably became more formalised. The age of the cricketing professional begins at about the same time that factory labour on a massive scale becomes institutionalised, but professional cricketers enjoyed the kinds of freedom workers in the mines or at the mill could only dream of. And not simply because work conditions were much better and the working day shorter. Playing cricket in cold and rain might not be comfortable, but it was preferable to crouching in a mine shaft or hunching over a loom; and a day of some ten hours spent in the open air was preferable by far to ten hours in the close, fetid, and often illness-inducing conditions of factory or pit. Moreover, cricketing professionals might not be well paid by their immediate employers, but they were to some extent free to take on other work, and, as MCC Tours began – which they did with increased frequency as the century progressed – and as private tour parties under rich benefactors also became fashionable – so the more gifted cricketers could expect to fill their pockets and bellies on a regular basis.

Cricket was the national sport. As nowadays there is a seemingly endless supply of football competitions, both domestic and international, so in the nineteenth century the developing County Championship was joined by a variety of competitive matches – Invitation X1s, including all-England teams, teams put out by titled gentlemen and/or rich landowners; and, of course, teams raised by cricketers whose prowess and fame guaranteed good gate money.

It would be irrelevant here to go into any detail regarding this burgeoning passion for competitive cricket – including tours both by MCC teams and privately funded parties. But it is at least necessary to remark that shamateurism is an inevitable part of the development of the domestic game. To take a well-known example. The United South of England team was set up by W.G. Grace with his lesser-known brother, E.M. A fee of £100 might be negotiated to cover the entire team for a three-day match. Each of the professionals the brothers employed would receive £5 for their work. The Two Graces pocketed the rest of the money. Well, it could be said, that was their business.

But that kind of business was something the brothers carried over into the county game, which is where matters become a good deal trickier. In 1846 the West Gloucester Cricket Club became Gloucester County Cricket Club. It played its first County match in 1870, against Surrey. WG, E.M, and the third brother, Fred Grace, were all in the team. Inevitably W.G. was captain and rather less inevitably E.M. acted as club secretary. Although the brothers were Gentlemen and therefore received no wages for playing cricket, a good deal of money found its way into their pockets as "expenses." There were protests as details of these generous reimbursements leaked out. The County Committee professed itself outraged at arrangements with which it was in fact in cahoots. These arrangements, they promised, would be regularised.

And how! The all-powerful W.G. retained the captaincy and a Finance Committee was set up to oversee the amount of money E.M. continued to trouser for himself and his siblings. Such decisive treatment pointed the way for other County Committees to promote the kind of shamateurism that survived into the early 1960s. Gentlemen were appointed to the captaincy of county sides. Gentlemen were also given salaried posts within the County structure. And Gentlemen could, and did, expect to receive generous expenses for giving their cricketing services for free.

It is hardly surprising, then, that many professional cricketers were resentful of the meagre wages they themselves received, especially as they often had to pay their own expenses. Mutterings of protest were inevitable, especially when we reflect that travel, lodging-house and occasional doctor's bills, plus money for kit, all routinely came from the little money the game offered the Players. It is this which helps to explain the recalcitrance of professional cricketers like Arthur Shrewsbury and Alfred Shaw. If the labourer was worthy of his hire, then they would see to it that as far as possible they were paid what they knew they were worth.

Not that their protests on behalf of better financial rewards for their cricketing labours were widely shared or, anyway, acted on. At all events, there is no evidence of rebellion against financial hardship ever rising to general visibility among cricketers before the First World War; and not all "shamateurs" did well out of the game. Neville Cardus's favourite, A.C. MacLaren, was usually short of the readies. W.G. Grace, who like MacLaren had no private means, was generous with his money, often treating poor patients without demanding a fee; and he would also travel miles for comparatively little in order to bring in spectators to a match from which others stood to make the money. *Admission 6d. If W.G. Grace plays Admission 1/3d.* So the hoardings outside many a cricket ground at the time were said to proclaim.

But open-handed as he may have been, Grace did well out of cricket, and this was certainly not the case for the majority of professionals. As William Gunn and others pointed out at the time, and as later commentators have also noted, professional cricketers in the nineteenth century had no great security of contract, the money they earned from cricket was little enough, during the winter months they were mostly required to fettle for themselves, and in later life they might well find themselves living in penury.

In view of all this, it may at first blush seem surprising that there wasn't some organised attempt among cricketers to negotiate better contractual terms. But as future chapters show, there are good reasons to explain why this was for so long delayed. One is that MCC control continued strong. Another is that this control was made possible because of the very nature of cricket and, of course, of cricketers. Militancy isn't often found in a game which seems to have at its core an ethos of loyalty, of willingness to serve the cause of cricket no matter how great the provocation to rebel against perceived injustices. If cricket is, or anyway was, the national game, then it makes sense to observe the in-built tendency to deference as a national trait. The rich man at his castle, The poor man at his gate; God made them high and lowly, And ordered their Estate. Rich men's estates for long supported County Cricket. Poor men entered through the Player's gate onto the cricket field.

Inevitably, some grumbled at this. But grumbling is what takes place after the match, in the bar. Once you are on the pitch, you get on with the game. You do what your Gentleman captain tells you. In the long years leading up to the First World War, and especially during cricket's so-called "Golden Age" – which roughly coincides with the years 1900-1914 – cricket could be seen as not merely the national sport but the sport that defined or typified a peacable nation, the contented acceptance of its class structures echoed in the game itself. And notwithstanding examples of rebellious behaviour in the nineteenth century – behaviour directed sometimes against the Laws of cricket, sometimes against the way it was financed, sometimes against the very idea of it being a team sport – the image of cricket as socially cohesive prevailed.

CODA

In his Introduction to the 1982 Oxford paperback edition of Hugh De Selincourt's novel, *The Game of the Season,* first published in 1931, John Arlott provides a superb account of the architectural design of the typical cricket pavilions built for gentlemen's country estates, pavilions which very clearly derived many features from those of great Test match grounds such as Lord's or Trent Bridge and which, between them, reveal the assumptions dictating their design.

> Unmistakeably Edwardian – or late Victorian – in style, red brick, gabled, and plentifully windowed, they might be three stories high. The basement was the groundsman's, with rollers, mowers, nets and assorted tools. The ground floor, where the teams normally took tea, was often used for dancing after play. On the first were the dressing-rooms and baths; the second, store-rooms and the scorers' Box with a wide window for the boys who manned the scoreboard. It was an aspect of a benignly feudal state: the most tolerant, expansive, light-hearted and pleasurable cricket man has ever known.

To this I would add only that the amount of rustication that was a feature of many of these pavilions adds to the sense of rural circumstance, one that strengthens the visual allusion to a benign feudal state. Arlott in no way discounts the appeal of this. But he also knows that, genuinely benign as it often was, or at all events considered itself to be, if it were to survive it had to rely on acceptance of its benignity by all concerned. Once that was doubted, or discovered to be more show than reality, then trouble was bound to ensue. And isn't shamateurism a form of pretending to the reality of something which, put to the test, turns out to be mere show? This being so, we can hardly be surprised if Players expressed discontent with what may have been less than a system but more than an occasional device to put money in the pockets of those who nevertheless continued to regard themselves as Gentlemen. From such rooted discontent, something akin to rebellion could well spread, though this is not to say that it inevitably did so. It is, though, to say that within the benign feudal state of cricket were a number of those whom it would be wrong to dismiss as mere malcontents.

Hitherto, *The Awkward Squad* has been concerned with cricket in the long period up to the onset of war in 1914. There were moments of rebellion in that by and large peacable period, though we have seen that these were dealt with either by accommodation – raising of wages, for example, modifying or altering Laws – or, occasionally, by ejecting from the peacable kingdom such mavericks as Billy Barnes and Bobby Peel, who, along with one or two others not mentioned in the present narrative, could be isolated as trouble-makers, fingered as malcontents, no more nor less, rebels acting without good cause, and who, once they were on the outside, found few sympathisers, even if Peel was able to continue making some money from the game. Nor was Barnes without his supporters. But these supporters had no power. That belonged to Notts CCC, and, in all senses of the word, they knew they could afford to use it.

And yet the consequences of the Great War, as it soon became called, with its millions of deaths, the vast social upheavals it inaugurated or hastened, would, we might reasonably assume, abut on cricket. The wonder, perhaps is, that for all the upheavals the events of 1914-18 produced, political, social, cultural, cricket seemed remarkable immune from most of them.

Business as usual, then? Perhaps. Or perhaps not.

Chapter 7: The Rural Scene

Derek Birley observes that as the Great War went on so, inevitably, large numbers of the pre-1914 generation of cricketers were among the thousands upon thousands of British troops killed in action or incapacitated from future engagement. These included many officers who, as first-class cricketing amateurs, were influential in the game. "These who succeeded them," Birley adds, "were, almost by definition, less secure in their convictions and though some were rebellious and cynical none sought to change society through cricket or sought to change cricket through itself." (p 211.)

Birley is almost certainly right to imply that cricketers among the officer-class were unlikely to feel especially rebellious towards either game or society, and the reasons are not difficult to find. In all the millions of words that have been written about The Great War there is wide agreement that, in England at least, there existed a strong desire to preserve a way of life seen as threatened by events on the continent of Europe. This was what English troops were meant to be fighting for. They were not in arms to change the world, but to preserve the one they had. When in 1915 Sir Maurice Yapp wrote the Introduction to a

YMCA anthology of English writings intended for troops going off to the front, he expressed his confidence that all soldiers would enjoy the contents. These would, he said, allow each reader "in imagination ... to see his village home." The anthology was called *The Old Country*.

There is an obvious oddity about this identification of England as a rural society. By then, most people were living in towns and cities. There is therefore also an oddity about assuming that troops who went off to war from Wales, Scotland and Northern Ireland, would be keen to identify the cause they were fighting for with rural England. As for those who came from London, Leeds, Leicester, Liverpool, or any of the industrial heartlands, what was rural England to them? Most men who volunteered, as well as those who were later conscripted, were leaving behind them social circumstances entirely different from the ones to which Yapp appeals. As social historians have pointed out, the years leading up to the war were characterised by strikes, mass unemployment, and widespread poverty. True, unemployment and poverty were common features of rural England, but this can hardly be what Yapp and those like him had in mind when they spoke of the "old country."

There undoubtedly was a nostalgic impetus behind those wanting to retain as much of The Old Country as might be possible. The war offered proof of the malign effects of modernity: of mass action created by mass civilization; it denied individuality, it took away not merely actual peace but the sweet sounds of the countryside. Soldiers waiting to go over the top in yet one more futile attack would hear, in the sudden cessation of artillery bombardments – a silence presaging the order to advance – the song of the skylark. The contrast was almost traumatisingly complete: on the one hand, the cacophonous sounds of war, on the other, the sound of pastoral innocence.

What could be more innocent than cricket? What more pastoral? What could be more *English*? Here, if anywhere, was to be found that benign feudal state which John Arlott detected in the architecture of cricket pavilions. Birley is surely right to suggest that those of the officer class who were at all concerned with cricket, either in playing or administering the game, had no desire to change it. "When this bleedin' war is over/And England once again at peace,/ We'll be strolling through the clover,/Watching batsmen at the crease." If anything, they wanted it preserved in amber, or, to shift the figure of speech, returned to that pre-war period which was soon – and how telling the term is – being identified as cricket's "Golden Age."

Any threat to that age had therefore to be countered, or denied, or, if all else failed, simply ignored. This almost certainly explains the appearance of so much writing about cricket in the period which does its best to wrap the game in a haze of comic, pastoral, innocence. P.G. Wodehouse hardly needs to be mentioned in this context. Ernest Raymond's *Tell England* (1922), however, is now forgotten, though at the time it was a huge best seller. Set at a public-school during the Great War, the novel includes a lengthy episode in which a comic cricket match importantly reminds us of the essential fair-minded decency of those about to go off to fight. And in the same year, 1922, a novel by Herbert Heyens, *Play Up Queens,* similarly uses a cricket match to establish the credentials of those who play.

The fictional presentation of village cricket as the opportunity of broad comedy becomes a marked feature of popular fiction in the 1920s and 30s, one that is so prevalent as almost to count as a sub-genre. And like all such sub-genres it has its rules. The weather will, against the odds, be good. Skullduggery or attempts to nobble matches will be incompetent, attempted by the opposition, and in the hands of those who are not true Gentlemen. All participants answer to expectation. Blacksmiths bowl fast but wildly, vicars can't catch, willowy young men sometimes display remarkable cowardice and on other occasions bat with supple ease; and young ladies are in love with the most dashing of the cricketers. (Who will certainly be a batsman.) Like stage comedies of the period, comic writing about cricket endorses the status quo. The village is the microcosm of English life, a place where social relations are understood and rank accepted by all. There are no serious malcontents, only the occasional (comic) drunkard. This is Housman's land of lost content given a new lease of life through the agency of fiction. There is no need to say more about it here, but interested readers may wish to consult the bibliography of *Lords & Commons: Cricket in Novels and Stories,* ed. John Bright-Holmes. (1988.)

Or they may consult Tim Heald's *Village Cricket.* (2004.) In the Introduction to his book, one of several he has written about the game, Heald remarks that "'Village' and 'cricket' are two of the most emotive words in the English language." Not if you're not interested in either, it has to be said, and there are plenty who aren't. Heald would not wish to credit this indifference or, for some, positive dislike of cricket and/or rural life. Because according to him, "The village is where, in an ideal world, most of us would like to live." By this he must mean that in an ideal world most of us would be living in villages. A village would mean "community, good neighbours, warmth, friendliness and a pervading sense of well-being. ... For those who believe in it the English village is Utopia."

And in this Utopia the only game that matters is cricket. Cricket connotes, so Heald assures us, "stiff upper lips, straight bats on sticky wickets, fair play and 'It matters not who won or lost but how you played the game.' ... for those who believe in it cricket is the true English religion." As a clincher Heald quotes the claim of the social historian G.M. Trevelyan that "If the French *noblesse* had been capable of playing cricket with their peasants, their chateaux would never have been burnt."

And if Charles 1st had played cricket with the new Model Army he wouldn't have lost his head. For all Heald's hint of comic deprecation in his account of village cricket, there is little doubt that he sees rural life as providing a model for good living.

Well, maybe, but then how account for the Swing Riots? To be fair to Heald, he sometimes comes near to acknowledging that the dream landscape of *Village Cricket* is tantamount to a nostalgia for some prelapsarian idyll whose simulacrum is not so much Utopia as the Land of Nod. Besides, if cricket is the true English religion for those who believe in it, it follows that by the 1980s, when Heald's book appeared, the majority of English people were backing some other religion, given that cricket was by then nowhere near as popular as football. And football is a sport primarily located in towns and cities.

Heald's sentimental view goes with a conservatism which spells death for the game he claims to love. It's a lost cause. Even John Major, for all his waffling on about George Orwell's dream of an England defined by misty meadows, warm beer, and spinsters cycling to church down twisty lanes – a dream which Orwell, writing in

1940, knew very well was, if not a mere dream, then very far from the whole truth – even Major, born in working-class South London, knows better than to confuse his evocation of pastoral England with reality. His favourite cricketing arenas are after all the Oval, home to Surrey CCC of which he has for years been president and where there is a John Major Room, and Lord's, and nobody is likely to mistake either of these for a village ground.

Yet through the centuries, cricket in England has been associated with a conservative view of society. Hence, the accuracy of Arlott's account of those pavilions associated with country house cricket, referred to in the previous chapter.

This account, as well as being a wonderfully astute reading of the social implications of pavilion architecture, acknowledges the charms of an idealised "benignly feudal state," though Arlott fully understands that it not only had comparatively little purchase in twentieth-century England, but that it was customarily honoured in the breach. And in the years after the Great War the emphasis on the "unchangeable" nature of cricket, especially but by no means only in fiction, has in common with most forms of pastoralism a rather desperate air of wish-fulfilment. If only it were *really* like this. In a sense, the image of village cricket, of settled, pastoral values, is very similar to the function of pre-Commonwealth Court Masque in the 17th century. And as Masque was played out in the awareness of gathering forces of opposition, so the image of cricket as a representation of permanent, unchangeable "Englishness," was being insisted on at a time when this image was beginning to look decidedly vulnerable. There might not be a Cromwell lurking in the shadows, but there was reason to fear the rise of village Hampdens. Or, bearing in mind what has just been said, of town and city

Hampdens. As Arlott observes, "For good or ill, the Engish village as a self-contained entity ceased to exist between the wars."

Chapter 8: Changing Times

The idealised image of cricket as the great stabiliser, outlined in the previous chapter, one that promotes the desirability of keeping things as they are, clearly goes with a fear of change. Change threatens the old order. Change is disruptive. Change is therefore bad. Those who were against change set themselves to remove it before it could set down roots. Change, they liked to say, constituted a rebellion against the very *nature* of cricket.

An unstated but taken-for-granted assumption in the resistance to change is that it wasn't merely not cricket. Such resistance wasn't English. Birley, who writes brilliantly about this, provides an intriguing example of what might be called the Rearguard position when he quotes from an article written in 1922 by Lord Harris for *The Cricketer*. The article is headed THE EFFECTS OF BOLSHEVISM and concerns slanders against the noble Lord that arose from his alleged attempts to recruit for Kent some players whose residential qualifications were at best questionable. Harris's behaviour drew the charge of hypocrisy. This is hardly surprising, given that as an influential member of the MCC he had been ardent in pursuit of other counties attempting to poach players with questionable residential qualifications.

But Bolshevism? A little extreme, perhaps, but in the closed world of cricket Harris no doubt saw any attempt to question his authority as an act of rebellion similar to, and perhaps even prompted by, what had happened in Russia in 1917. Overthrow the tsar of cricket and who knew what discord might follow? The Communist Party of Great Britain had been established in 1920, which was the year when dockers refused to load ships with arms intended for Russia's White Army, a year in which *The Daily Herald* became the preferred newspaper for millions of working-class readers, and when the Communist newspaper, the *Worker,* became a daily, in which the Labour Party gave clear evidence of a massive increase in voting strength – evidence that became palpable when, two years after Harris detected Bolshevism in the murky backwaters of cricket, a Labour government came into office (admittedly a minority one, and one that didn't last for long, but still). And 1922, besides being the year of *Tell England* and *Play Up Queens,* and Harris's declaration, was also the year of *The Waste Land* and *Ulysses* (admittedly, not works with which Harris is likely to have rushed to acquaint himself, though had he known of them he might well have seen them as straws in the revolutionary wind), and of mass marches of the unemployed.

"MCC were scarcely the organisation to encourage radicalism," Birley wryly notes (p 212), but for all the insistence on things being as they had always been – which of course meant pretending that the past was a good deal more golden than its actual colour – the old guard faced the future with some trepidation. Hence, almost certainly, Warner's founding of *The Cricketer* in 1921. Warner was by then cricketing correspondent of the *Morning Post,* "the stoutest pillar of respectability," according to Birley, and *The Cricketer* "was a sort of sporting equivalent. Its first issue made it clear that this was to be no alternative or rabble-rousing sheet." As conclusive evidence of this, Birley quotes from the words Warner hammered to the mast. "Cricket, as Tom Brown has told us in the best of all school stories, is an institution and the habeas corpus of every boy of British birth." (p 215.) This might be called Warner's False Syllogism. All British boys take cricket to be their birthright. Any boy who claims to be British and who does not like cricket is therefore not British, the reason being that he has not attended public school. Alternatively, all British boys have been to public school, therefore boys who have not done so are not British. Worse, they must be *anti*-British. Q.E.D.

In view of this, it is intriguing to note that the term Bolshevism soon found a place in Warner's fairly limited vocabulary. Even when he was making, in Birley's words, a ponderous joke of denying that there were undue delays in appointing a captain to face the 1921 touring Australians, he explained that such delays as there were could not be explained as "a brilliant Bolshevik move on the part of the players." (p 217.) How we laughed.

But such a move was to be feared. Gentlemen in England must be out of their beds and ready to face the enemy within. As Birley also points out, when in 1924 Cecil Parkin queried the worth of A.E.R. Gilligan as England captain, Warner was incensed. He wrote an article in *The Cricketer* demanding that Parkin apologise and that his county, Lancashire, take action against him. Parkin, Warner fulminated, "would be the first cricketing Bolshevik", and the cricket world would surely have none of him. Lancashire CCC took Warner's dire warning seriously. In 1926 Parkin was sacked. No Bolsehviks at Old Trafford, thank you very much.

Neville Cardus says nothing of this nastiness in his appreciation of Parkin in *Cricket All the Year*. (1952.) "One of those cricketers whose spirit, humour and whimsy transcend a game and make them storm the hearts of people not at all technically instructed," he says, and he goes on to extol Parkin the bowler, "Tall, snapdragon, Jack Ketch and Merry Andrew, with a break-back, bowled round the wicket on 'sticky' pitches, so acute in angle, so vicious in 'kick', that the leg-trap did its work like body-snatchers." Cardus then tells some anecdotes about Parkin as a batsman, as a crowd pleaser, and ends his encomium by calling him "A fellow of jest sadly finite! Witty, humorous, herald of the approaching times of irreverence and disrule, and all the more lovable for his delinquencies. A source of happiness to countless Lancashire men and women, and Lancashire lads and lasses. May the soil rest lightly on him." (pp 39-41)

"Herald of the approaching times of irreverence and disrule." This is presumably a coy allusion to the contretemps that led to Parkin being kicked out by Lancashire, though it feels remarkably pusillanimous of Cardus to tell us that Parkin was all the more lovable for his "delinquencies" without uttering at least a word of criticism against those responsible for ridding themselves of this "source of happiness." Mightn't they be held to account? Besides, what exactly does Parkin's insubordination herald? Cardus is after all writing long after Lancashire's sacking of an outstanding cricketer, one of the finest bowlers of his generation. Does he have in mind the Bodyline controversy or is this his way of hinting at other, wider discontents?

If so, he doesn't sympathise with those who express them: "irreverence and disrule" is the language of a man trying to recall Ulysses' speech in *Troilus and Cressida,* it's the utterance of someone very clearly on the side of those in authority who proclaim the dire consequences of taking degree away, untuning the string. Do that, and you have a full-blown rebellion on your hands. Better to stamp out the flames before they can spread. For all his praise of Parkin, Cardus sees no reason to defend him against Warner's imputation, and this seems to me typical of both of them and the type of thinking they represent. Warner liked to present himself as someone of lordly good will to all cricketers. As long, that is, as they did his bidding, saw matters his way. If they didn't they were a contaminant from which cricket must be protected. As for Cardus, rebels were to be treated as "characters". Loveable but not to be taken seriously. What right has Parkin, a mere professional, Warner implies, to dare to criticise Gilligan. And Cardus as good as answers, yes, I quite understand your irritation, but he's only a player, so there's no great need to get hot under the collar over his silly remarks.

* * *

As no follower of cricket surely needs reminding, Warner was used to getting his own way. There was to be no discord on his watch. He was also adept in hiding behind others when his way turned out to be wrong or to lead to unforeseen consequences, especially if these in any way threatened to expose him to criticism. In 1921 he was one of those who appointed J.W.H.T. Douglas to captain England against Australia in the series the Australians won by three matches, with two drawn. Birley says that although there were legitimate excuses for England's poor performance, including the absence of Hobbs and Hearne, there can be none for what he calls the "hand-to-mouth amateurism of the selectors and their old-boy network." (p 218.) Oddly, for so perspicacious and knowledgeable an historian of the game, he doesn't mention that George Gunn was never chosen to play against an Australian team which included Gregory and McDonald, even though Gunn had a spectacularly good year for Notts and that, looking back to the year in *Cricket's Secret History,* Walter Hammond noted that "When Gregory and McDonald scythed their way through the crop of English wickets, some batsmen, among whom I frankly admit I was one, were afraid of them ... Only George Gunn plainly enjoyed them." (Quoted in *The Trent Bridge Battery: The Story of the Sporting Gunns,* Haynes & Lucas, 1985.)

The English selectors tried no fewer than thirty players that summer, but George Gunn was not once called on. The explanation for this extraordinary omission of one of the finest batsman of his age from a team desperately in need of a good opener seems to be that Warner thought, and said, that Gunn stood too much in front of his wicket. George Gunn was certainly liable to bat in an unorthodox manner, though when occasion demanded it he was exquisitely correct. But in his *Book of Cricket,* first published in 1911, and throughout the years regularly re-printed, Warner opined that although batsmen are free to choose the stance most natural to them, and that "no fixed rules can be laid down as to the position a batsman should take up at the wicket," standing in front of them is not a good idea. Nor is carrying a heavy bat. "It is a thousand times better to play with too light a bat than too heavy a one." George Gunn, who famously used a bat that was at least two pounds, six ounces (the average bat was four ounces fewer), therefore offended on two fronts. A bit of a Bolshevik, then.

Well, no, not really. But if not a natural rebel, nor openly mutinous, George Gunn was undoubtedly a cricketer who enjoyed going his own way, and he didn't take kindly to being ordered about by those he could find no great reason to respect. From the first he was contrary. He declared independence of his own family connections when choosing to use bats that had not been manufactured by Gunn and Moore, the firm of sports suppliers which his uncle, the great William Gunn, had founded. George Gunn was invariably mild in manner, usually courteous, and utterly self-willed. There is the story of how, when an experimental Law came in for the taking of lunch at later than 1.30pm., George, who for some reason had not been made aware of the change – perhaps he simply couldn't credit what he was told – and who was called back to the crease as he began to make his way to the pavilion after his morning's work, returned, took up arms, then, as the bowler delivered the first ball of a new over, stepped aside, allowed himself to be castled, tucked his bat under his arm, said, "I take my lunch at 1.30pm," and left the field. It is probably an apocryphal tale, but that it should have been attributed to him tells us much about the man.

The focus here, though, is less on George Gunn than on Warner. Warner's dyed-in-the-wool Establishment ways, his taken-for-granted assumption that his views were beyond question, inevitably riled others, turning at least some of them into rebels. Being criticised by an infinitely less gifted cricketer cannot have endeared Warner to Gunn, any more than his unorthodox batting endeared him to Warner.

Nor can Gunn's readiness to speak out of turn have done him much good at Lord's. In his memoir, *46 Not Out*, (1948), R.C. Robertson-Glasgow recalls a Festival match played at Blackpool in 1924 when the umpires were instructed to be "very generous about LBW decisions." Robertson-Glasgow notes that "George Gunn, sidling up from mid-on, said to one of the umpires 'and I suppose if anyone's bowled (rhyming with 'scowled') it's just a nusty accident?'" Admittedly, the fact of this being a Festival match made bearable what might otherwise have viewed as a Player getting a bit above himself. But Gunn was never a great one for tugging his forelock.

The issue here is perhaps less unorthodoxy, let alone a refusal to go by the book, than the challenge by Players to Gentlemen which such a refusal implies. Gilbert Jessop – "the Croucher" – was no great exemplar of Warner's belief in proper batting style. But Jessop was a Gentleman. George Gunn wasn't.

Nor, for that matter, was Philip Mead (1887-1958). The left-handed Mead, who was Hampshire's opening batsman and a slow left-arm bowler for thirty years, from 1905-1336, hit a thousand runs in a season on as many as 27 occasions, and in 1921 scored no fewer than 3,179 runs, at an average of 69.10. "In the opinion of many he was considered unlucky not to obtain a regular place in the England team." Thus, the *Who's Who of Cricketers*.

But Mead, who, it should perhaps be noted, played in the Festival match mentioned above, had a decidedly unorthodox way of batting. Film at Trent Bridge, shot in the early 1920s, shows him waiting to face the bowling and, as the bowler runs up the wicket, Mead, who has been standing well to the leg-side of the pitch, shuffles into his crease and is in position a mere fraction of a second, so it seems, before the bowler sends down his delivery. Not a model of stillness, then.

However, in *Cricket Prints* (1943), R. C. Robertson-Glasgow, who bowled against him often enough, gives a rather different impression. He does not award Mead all that many marks for an attractive style. "He took guard with the air of a guest who, having been offered a week-end by his host, obstinately decides to reside for six months. Having settled his whereabouts with the umpire, he wiggled the toe of his left boot for some fifteen seconds inside the crease, pulled the peak of a cap that seemed all peak, wiggled again, pulled again, then gave a comprehensive stare around him ... Then he leaned forward and looked at you down the pitch, quite still." And Robertson-Glasgow adds that although Mead could play all the strokes, "without frill or fancy," for the most part "he avoided adventure because he could prosper without it." Which Mead certainly did. "Hants. Wickets fall. But Mead still batting," Robertson-Glasgow records the back-page headline of a daily newspaper as encapsulating Mead's career. (p 37)

His fidgetiness was legendary. The Australian cricket writer Ray Robinson records in *Between Wickets* (1946) that Mead was a champion "peak fingerer." (see pp 147-8.) He was also capable of batting with a kind of granitic obduracy. There is a story that during a match Hampshire were playing at Lord's against Middlesex, his county captain, Lionel, Lord Tennyson, was at his London club soaking out the effect of the previous night's champagne when he was sent news of Mead's slow progress. Tennyson dispatched a telegram to the ground which was carried out to Mead on a silver salver borne by Tennyson's butler. The telegram read **Mead Get Out. Tennyson.** Mead put the telegram in his back pocket and carried on batting.

But Tennyson must have valued Mead's batting rather more than he disliked his rebellious obduracy, because he took him on tour to Jamaica in 1927/8, and Mead also went on MCC tours to Australia in 1911/12 and, much later, 1928/9, as well as tours to South Africa in 1913/14 and again in 1922/3. Nevertheless, his appearances for England were remarkably few, and it is difficult to avoid the conclusion that, like Gunn, his face didn't fit or, to speak rather more accurately, his style didn't suit. And this, though Warner himself in *Cricket Between Two Wars* (1942) admits that Mead was one of the few successes of the 1921 debacle. "Amidst all the shortcomings and disappointments Woolley's two glorious innings of 95 and 93, at Lord's will be remembered as long as there is a history of cricket, and Mead, who made 47 at Old Trafford and 182 not out at the Oval…" (p 5)

Moreover, Warner was one of the Selectors who, so he says, chose Mead to go on the 1928/9 Australian tour, following a summer in which the Hampshire opener scored 3027 runs at an average of 75.67. Yet Mead only played in the first Test, when he scored 8 and 73. It's difficult to know from this whether Warner was for, against, or impartial. Given Mead's form in 1928 it would have been virtually impossible to omit him from the touring party; Warner's hand may well have been forced.

But after that one Test Mead was dropped. The selectors apparently decided that for the next Test they needed an extra bowler, and it being inconceivable that any of Hobbs, Sutcliffe, Hammond, Jardine or Hendren could be sacrificed, and as the captain, Percy Chapman, was yet another batsman, Mead had to stand aside.

(England won the first Test by 675 runs so they could reasonably feel assured that even without Mead they had enough batting to be going on with.) Moreover, Woolley was omitted from the touring party – "After much cut and thrust in debate – always conducted with dignity and even temper," Warner says, and the other left-hander, Leyland, played only in the last Test, "where he covered himself with glory with innings of 137 and 53 not out."

Warner shimmies away from the responsibility of having omitted Woolley. "Looking back across the years, it seems extraordinary that he should have been omitted, and I can recall words of Gerry Weighall which still sting. That great pundit was beside himself with rage and likened Leyland to a 'cross-bat village greener,' while Woolley he likened to a god; and an anonymous letter-writer described Mead as a 'leaden-footed carthorse.'" (p 65.)

It might be expected that Warner would want to defend both batsmen against such clumsy bludgeoning. After all, he'd been of the selectorial party, and scores of 8 and 73 and 137 and 53 n.o. hardly amount to failure by either Mead or Leyland. But no. Not a word is said on their behalf. We are, it seems certain, intended to infer that Warner was outvoted in his preference for Woolley, especially as a little later he adds that "Whether the team … was the best possible must, as is generally the case, be a matter of opinion, but, excepting the omission of Woolley, it was well received and inspired confidence." (p 66.)

The impression given here as by so much of Warner's writing and behaviour is of someone who is taking infinite pains never to be found accountable for making the wrong decision, who wants to be all things to all men, who is Simon Pure. Hence, the distrust, even contempt, in which he was widely held by cricketers of the time. There is, to take a single example, the story, told by David Foot in his *Cricket's Unholy Trinity* (1985), of the occasion when Charlie Parker (1882-1959), Gloucestershire's left-arm slow bowler, who was only once chosen to play for England despite regularly taking over 100 wickets a season in a playing career that began in 1903 and ended over thirty years later, was so incensed at overhearing Warner complain in a West country hotel about the current dearth of good slow bowling in England, that he grabbed him by the lapels in a rage of protest, shook him violently, and was assured that he would never play for England again. But then Parker, a more obstreperous cricketer than either Gunn or Mead – well, he was a bowler – did not welcome criticism from anyone. Notoriously averse from pursuing a ball hit anywhere near him, he would insist, "I'm a bowler, not a bleedin' fielder." Small wonder then that when, as he assumed, his skills as a bowler were being slighted, he nearly shook the life out of Warner. That act of rebellion against Mr Smooth did for Parker's international career, for once and for all, but it probably made him feel better.

* * *

The reason for spending time on Warner is because, in the inter-war period, the role of selectors in choosing Test teams inevitably became more of an issue than in former times. In earlier days, team selection was a matter for the CCCs of grounds where the Test match was to be played. But as Lord's assumed control, as the governance of the game became more centralised, so those who ruled at Lord's became of prime significance. A great deal more was now at stake for professional cricketers whose livelihoods as well as pride were bound up with selection for or rejection from the national side. To be at the mercy or whim of those who take for granted their right to decide your fate is not pleasant. In their different ways, Parkin, Gunn, and Mead, as well as a host of others, could hardly not have felt resentment at the treatment handed out to them by Warner and his ilk. And this being so, it is inconceivable that they did not let their feelings be known to others. Such voiced or muttered resentment might not amount to Bolshevism, but in the minds of those who saw themselves as the cricket's unquestionable masters the merest whisper of discontent could well seem to be borne on the poison breath of insubordination, of "irreverence and disrule."

The point isn't one to labour, but cricketers of the inter-war period did after all live in a society where hunger marches, protest rallies and, once, a General Strike, indicated the large scale discontent of millions of men and women, among whom, we should remember, professional cricketers lived as neighbours, friends, family members. Cricketers may be "naturally" conservative or, as John Arlott would call them, "romantics". They were prepared to put up with much because of their love for the game they played – a love that had within it a sizeable amount of stoical, uncomplaining acceptance of their lot. When they grumbled it was therefore mostly about the weather or the state of the pitch or changing-room facilities, or some other element that was part of what could be thought of as the daily ritual of licensed complaint.

But there were other, larger, matters that tested their patience, and which, for some at least, bred a genuine rebelliousness. This has a bearing on what comes next.

Chapter 9: Rebels and Loyalists

To say that cricketers as a whole rather than merely the professionals among them distrusted Warner may seem excessive. Surely the Gentlemen, among whom he considered himself *primus inter pares,* would harbour no doubts? But some of them did. And to explain this and the rebellion that he both occasioned and out of which Warner made further rebels, brings us, inevitably, to what is still probably the most famous of all cricketing controversies, Body Line or, as it is often called, Bodyline.

This may appear to overstate the case. It's at least arguable that Bodyline attracted no more attention in its time than the wide-spread and prolonged debate of the 1970s about what became known as The Packer Affair. Kerry Packer was undoubtedly the cause of outrage among those who felt that with the World Series he opened the way to commercial exploitation of a game which ought to be above the lure of filthy lucre. Not only that: Packer was threatening to take control of cricket's interests from the hands of those who regarded themselves as its instituted authorities.

But in retrospect he and those who worked with him could be said to have been pushing at an at least half-open door. Packer's blatantly self-interested stunt – if the Series can be called that – led to a wide acceptance that cricket had to be better "marketed" if it was to survive in a world where other sports were doing a great deal better by and for those who played them. Cricketers needed to be decently paid, otherwise they would become lost to the game or play officially outlawed but financially rewarding versions; besides, the game itself needed to attract paying spectators, whether those paying did so at the turnstiles or via television. There had been a steady falling away of crowds from the vast numbers who watched cricket in the immediate post-war years. Now, the proverbial three men and a dog were as much as cricketers in county cricket matches could expect to watch, or so they laconically remarked. Once well-attended fixtures were played out in front of empty stands. Packer intended to change all that.

Or anyway, he wanted to change some things. And to a large extent he succeeded in doing as he intended. Although the Packer affair damaged one or two playing careers – most spectacularly, perhaps, it put an end to Tony Greig's days as an international cricketer – those who took Packer gold did well enough out of their decisions in later life. And it should be said that, perhaps as a direct consequence of Packer, the English "rebels" who toured South Africa at the beginning of the 1980s were, despite three-year bans, all re-absorbed into cricket, either as players and, later, coaches and MCC stalwarts (Gooch, Gatting), or commentators and "sages". (Boycott.) In other words, the controversy Packer caused died away as its effects were taken back into the game. And nobody involved either in his World Series or the reprehensible South African tours suffered greatly. Even Greig, who together with Richie Benaud emerged as Packer's arch-plotter – the Enemy Within, finished up as a TV commentator and pundit.

In steep contrast, the Bodyline controversy did lasting damage to many of those involved. Harold Larwood, one of the greatest fast bowlers of any time, never again played for England after the 1932-3 tour of Australia. Douglas Jardine, captain of the touring team and the man who thought up the idea of Bodyline, left the game entirely, Bill Voce was omitted from England's Test team for a number of years, the career of Arthur Carr as captain of Notts. was brought to an abrupt end as a direct consequence of his backing Larwood; whereas oleaginous specimens such as Warner and G.O. Allen slid away from harm. They had the power to do hurt, and they did it. But they themselves did not suffer.

Because so much has been written about the subject of Bodyline, most recently in Duncan Hamilton's full-dress biography, *Harold Larwood* (2009), it would be otiose to tell the story yet again. Instead, I hope to come at the familiar tale from a different angle, or, to shift metaphors, to pull free some threads from this much-entangled narrative of heroes, villains, loyalists, rebels, where national pride and national disgrace have been allowed to feature as constituent colours in some of the more elaborate, not to say, fanciful tapestries woven out of the events. But first, the background.

In 1930 the touring Australians won the Test series by two to England's one, with two Tests drawn. The outstanding, indeed dominant performer on either side was Donald Bradman, so much so, in fact, that the summer of 1930 became known as "Bradman's Tour." The statistics don't on this occasion lie. Bradman scored centuries in four of the five Tests, three of them over 200, one of 334. Herbert Sutcliffe topped the averages for England and his 87.20 may seem enviable until it is compared with Bradman's 139.14, more than 50 ahead of the Yorkshire opening batsman. England's leading wicket taker for the series was Maurice Tate, but his 15 wickets cost him 38.20 apiece, each of R.W.V. Robins's 10 averaged out at 33.80, and Larwood, who was ill on and off through the summer, finished with 4 wickets at 73.00.

For the first four tests England were captained by Percy Chapman, but he was deposed for the final Test, which was, as custom by then demanded, played at the Oval. According to Warner, Chapman was much at fault in allowing the Australians to score so freely in the four Tests for which he had responsibility over England's side. He set poor fields and sent his fast bowlers into the "country" to chase leather. Warner characteristically adds that "Ranji … could not begin to understand how a man who had had so much experience of leadership should have literally presented runs to his opponents." (*Cricket Between Two Wars,* p 88.)

So out went Chapman and in came R.E. S. Wyatt and a fat lot of good it did the home side, who were beaten by an innings and 39 runs, their worst defeat of the series. In fairness, it should be noted that in England's first innings Wyatt scored 64 runs; but in the second, when a captain's innings was much needed, he made only 7 before being bowled by Hornibrook.

Wyatt wasn't therefore the answer to England's problem, which was how to contain Bradman, in the Ashes series to be played Down Under, 1932-3. And with four Test wickets at 73 each in the summer of 1930, Larwood might not have been thought a shoe-in for selection, either.

But in 1932, restored to full fitness, he took 141 wickets in the championship at 11 apiece, and, having been primed by his captain as to how he would be expected to bowl during the upcoming series, he was included in the touring party that set sail for Australia in the late autumn, one of sixteen cricketers under the captaincy of Douglas Jardine, who was accompanied by two managers, R.C.N. Palairet and Warner. (Maurice Tate, who was ill when the party left, joined up with the rest a few weeks later at Sydney.)

Warner's summary of the tour and of Jardine's role is a faultless exercise in slippery evasion. Jardine, he tells us, "had many admirable qualities, and was as good a tactician as any captain I have ever seen." He set a good example of physical fitness, was unselfish, and "Especially was he a master in the art of changing the bowling and in keeping his bowlers fresh. As for Body Line, as the Australians called it, he thought that this type of bowling was legitimate and within the rules."

Warner, however, disagreed. "My own view is that it was wrong ethically and also tactically, and that Larwood often 'wasted his sweetness on the desert air' by sending down, for example, 39 out of 42 deliveries on the line of the batsmen, or just clear of him, as he did at Sydney in the first Test. …Admittedly, Larwood clean bowled a large proportion of his wickets, but then Larwood had complete control of the ball and would follow two or three bouncers with a good-length break ball or a yorker."

As indeed Larwood did. Of his 33 wickets, taken at a cost of 19.51 apiece, sixteen were bowled and two LBW. The next highest wicket-taker was G.O. "Gubby" Allen, with 21 wickets, and third came Larwood's Nottinghamshire fellow-

Sir Pelham Warner (above) and Sir Julian Cahn (below).

opening bowler, Bill Voce, who took 15. And this is where matters become contentious.

Here is Warner. "Allen never bowled Body Line, and, as *Wisden* put it, '...enjoyed many successes.' Surely, with his extra pace, Larwood could have done as well as Allen and avoided the bitter feeling." It is of course probable that more than one of Allen's successes occurred because, in their relief at being away from Larwood, batsman played with more freedom than was good for them, much as in the post-war era it was often suggested that quite a few of Trueman's wickets came about because batsmen relaxed once they were away from the relentless accuracy of Brian Statham, the bowler who regularly partnered Trueman in England's opening attack.

Nevertheless, the bitterness of the Australians at Boydyline is well-known and is probably best summed-up in Woodfull's famous dressing-room complaint during the Adelaide Test that "There are two teams out there. One is trying to play cricket and the other is not." This was after he'd been hit over the heart by a rising ball from Larwood and, following his dismissal – he was bowled by Allen – Warner had gone into the Australian dressing-room to apologise, only to be told "I don't want to see you, Mr Warner."

"One of the strongest arguments against [Body Line bowling] is that it breeds anger, hatred and malice, with consequent reprisals. The courtesy of combat goes out of the game." Thus Warner, who adds, however, that the ball which hit Woodfull was "on or just outside the off-stump," while Oldfield, who had to retire hurt having been hit on the head, "tried to hook a straight ball, got his feet in the wrong position [and] mistimed the stroke." (pp 127-8) In other words, neither injury was caused by Bodyline, though both were the result of batsmen unable to cope with the pace of a bowler Joe Hardstaff always insisted was the fastest he had ever seen or faced. And he only faced "Lol", as he called him, in the nets.

This is not to dispute the fact that Larwood and Voce were bowling to orders and that the man who gave them the orders, Jardine, had every intention of discomposing the Australians and getting them to surrender their wickets. Jardine was chosen to win back the Ashes. Given that England won by four Tests to one he can be said to have succeeded. But the success came at a price. Larwood, in particular, and Voce to a slightly lesser extent were to be heavily criticised for their tactics. Bodyline was widely condemned as unfair. It simply wasn't cricket. In *The Little Wonder: The Remarkable History of Wisden* (2013), Robert Winder gives the more or less orthodox account of the cause of bad feelings Bodyline generated among the Australians and subsequently in England, when he says that "Things came to a noisy head in the Third Test at Adelaide when Larwood first fractured Bert Oldfield's skull with a lifter, but still carried on the assault. It suggested a merciless streak not always linked with the old idea of fair play." (p 168.) Leaving aside the fact that, as we have seen, through the history of cricket "the old idea of fair play" had often been ignored or undermined by some dodge, this is inaccurate. Hamilton says that immediately after hitting Oldfield – who had been standing outside off stump – Larwood apologised to the batsman who replied "It's not your fault Harold, I was trying to hook you for four." And later, Oldfield apparently said "criticism of Larwood is unjust."

But wherever the truth may lie, there is no doubt that both bowler and captain became vilified for their deeds.

They had won the Ashes, but they had used dirty tricks to do so. So, months after the Ashes were gained, many agreed. At the time, though, English newspapers, and those of the public interested in the series, joined in celebrating the Ashes victory, and Larwood became something of a national hero. A photograph of a London street scene in February, 1933, reveals hoardings that proclaim **JARDINE on our VICTORY** (*Mid-Day Standard*) and **HOW WE WON THE ASHES FULL**

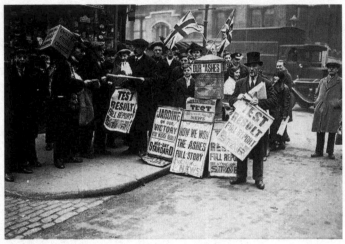

STORY (*Evening News*), and among the crowd shown buying newspapers two Union Jacks are waved aloft (below).

Jardine was the general who master-minded the victory. But to bring it about he needed Larwood and Voce to bowl to orders. In doing this so successfully, they did as England expected. They did their duty. If they were guilty of rebelling against the true spirit of the game, they were innocent of rebelling against authority – that of their captain. It is Allen, the amateur, who can be classed as a rebel for refusing to follow the tactics Jardine dreamed up, just as the amateur Nawab of Pataudi can be called rebellious for refusing to take his place in the leg trap. "I see his Highness is a conscientious objector," Jardine allegedly said when the Nawab declined to field where his captain wanted him to go.

Both Allen and the Nawab, of course, were eventually lauded by the Lord's establishment as having upheld the true spirit of cricket. Birley quotes a letter from Allen to his father, written from Australia, in which he remarked that "Douglas Jardine is loathed ... he is a perfect swine and I can think of no fit words for Mummy to see when I describe him." As for Larwood and Voce, they are "swollen-headed, gutless, uneducated miners." (*A Social History of English Cricket*, p 246.) Allen, Eton and Cambridge, and later CBE, who would become Chairman of the Test selectors from 1955-61 and treasurer of the MCC from 1964 until 1976, spoke for the Establishment.

In later years, perhaps fearful for his posthumous reputation, Allen used the opportunity provided by a study of the events surrounding Bodyline to cover his tracks. *The Bodyline Controversy* (1983), a fairly bland book by Laurence le Quesne, features a Foreword by Allen, who declares his belief that it is "the most impartial account of what took place and the repercussions that followed." Just how impartial le Quesne's book is can be gauged from the author's heavy reliance on Allen's testimony, which includes the following remarkable statement, in which Allen, having acknowledged more in sorrow than anger that, yes, he was hostile to Jardine's tactics, tells the author that nevertheless "he remained probably Jardine's closest friend throughout the tour." (p 31.) Le Quesne is presumably ignorant of Allen's letter home in which the tour captain is called "a perfect swine", so he has no reason to doubt Allen's words about being Jardine's friend. Nor is there any mention of

Larwood and Voce being gutless, uneducated miners. Allen emerges from le Quesne's book smelling of roses. The wise friend, the voice of the Establishment, enlightened, magnanimous, and, of course, right.

But this was later. At the time of the controversy, or anyway at a time he was still hoping to avert one, it was Warner who took it upon himself to speak for the Establishment as well as to it, when he claimed that, following his visit to the Australians' dressing-room to commiserate with Woodfull, he and the Australian captain had become "the best of friends." Unfortunately for him, his statement was fiercely denounced by Woodfull as soon as the Australian found out about Warner's diplomatic efforts. So Warner scuttled for cover. And from there he began his campaign to point the finger at Larwood, Voce, and the captain under whose direction they won the Ashes.

The fullest account of the treatment dished out to the two great bowlers is to be found in Duncan Hamilton's authorised, detailed and sympathetic biography of Larwood, referred to above. To repeat, Larwood never again played for England and Voce had to wait four years before he was recalled to the Test team. Both were understandably embittered by the way they were treated as a result of the tour, and in Voce's case at least the acid was still in his system when, fifty years later, the present author was working with Basil Haynes on *The Trent Bridge Battery* and, during a visit we paid to Joe Hardstaff, he phoned Bill Voce hoping to persuade his old team mate to allow us to talk to him. Voce refused point blank. He presumably thought we were yet more muck-rakers.

A pity, but understandable. Because soon after the touring party returned, the dirt began to fly. Not initially. Not only did the touring party arrive back to plaudits from the popular press, they even received a telegram of congratulations from the then Prime Minister, Ramsey MacDonald, not a known follower of cricket. But reaction soon set in. Fences were to be repaired. After all, the Australians were due in England the following year. Efforts were made to get Larwood in particular to apologise for his bowling. He refused. What on earth was he supposed to apologise *for*? He had done exactly as was asked of him by his captain, the tactics had worked, he had taken thirty-tree wickets, and England had won the Ashes. But the slide from hero to villain had begun.

While Larwood and Voce were being castigated, Jardine, who to his credit always championed them, seemed to have emerged unscathed. Having triumphed against the Australians he was re-appointed as England's captain for the 1933 season against the West Indies and again for the winter's tour of India. Given his triumph in the Ashes series, he could hardly *not* have been. But although in public Warner and others at Lord's might demonstrate their confidence in Jardine by continuing to appoint him to lead the national side, their private reflections were very different. Jardine was a loose cannon. The problem was how to roll him overboard before the Australians arrived for the 1934 tour. Were Jardine to be still captain for that Test series, intense bad feeling was guaranteed.

The weasels had one slice of luck. Larwood injured himself at the end of the Australian tour and so was unavailable for selection for the 1933 Test matches. That left the problem of what to do about Voce, who was fit. Still, there were other bowlers to choose among. Voce was expendable. He was owed no apology. He was therefore dropped.

So much for loyalty.

Chapter 10: Rebels For a Cause

The MCC, in a quandary about how to respond to the hostility of the Australians to Bodyline, had luck in their side. Larwood's injury in 1933 proved more serious than at first hoped (by Arthur Carr, his captain at Notts) or feared (by Lord's). As for Jardine, Warner *et al* were spared the problem of what to do about him when he declared himself unavailable for the 1934 season. A brave batsman, a skilled tactician, but intransigent, opinionated, and in some circumstances probably as unpleasant as his enemies said he always was – but given the nature of those enemies, he had reason enough – Jardine in all likelihood saw no reason to put up with Lord's and its devious ways. He had anyway nothing much to gain by staying on. Allen's "perfect swine" had behaved well by Larwood and Voce. They had done as he asked and he stood by them. When in June 1933 the people of Nottingham put together a sizeable cheque in recognition of the previous winter's achievements by their two great bowlers, it was Jardine who presented a cheque for £400 and a silver salver to each in a ceremony held on the balcony at Trent Bridge during a county match against Surrey.

But he must have known that by then he was becoming *persona non grata* at Lord's. He was loyalist turned rebel and those who served under him, by being loyal to him, were inevitably to be classed as rebels. All of them had, it was now agreed, besmirched the spirit of cricket. It was this devious logic which, as Hamilton and others have rightly noted, bewildered Larwood. It didn't bewilder Jardine. It simply stuck in his craw. Why bother? Accordingly, he stalked off to a life of business.

At which point their own county captain became important to the two bowlers. A.W. Carr (1893-1963) is a rare example of gamekeeper turned poacher. Born into a wealthy family, educated at Sherborne and Eton, he was a roisterer by inclination and something of a hell-raiser. Judging from photographs he can be said to incline to the Terry-Thomas side of Errol Flynn's looks, though without the moustache of either. When Basil Haynes and I were at work on our book about the Gunns we heard many stories of Carr's drinking habits. On one notorious occasion his three-wheeled Morgan became stuck in the doorway of a Nottingham pub whose bar he was trying to reach before last orders were called. He would, we were told, regularly turn up at the house of one or other of his team-mates in the early hours, shouting for them to join him in drinking whatever booze he happened to have by him. John Gunn in particular learned to dread the call.

But Carr as a cricketer was no slouch. He captained Notts from 1919 to 1934, during which time he scored 1,000 runs or more on eleven occasions, and in 1929 he finally led his team, who partly under his eye for latent talent and guidance had become one of the most powerful in the country, to the County Championship. That he was genuinely popular with his teams and supporters there can be no doubt. Wynne-Thomas reports that at the end of the summer of 1933, when he had completed fifteen years as Captain of Notts, 120 members of the County Club wrote an open letter to the press praising Carr for the way he had led the side that season. This was supported by a letter from Carr's team, who in what Wynne-Thomas calls "a most unusual response", wrote to "express our very deepest appreciation and gratitude to our Skipper for the splendid and untiring way he has captained the side this year. No man," they add, "could have done more than he has done, and the older members of the side, especially, realise what anxiety and worry this has entailed during what has been a most difficult season … We all thank Mr Carr from the bottom of our hearts for his guidance, counsel and friendship and hope that he may be spared many years to continue as the county's captain." (p 176.)

They may not have known of the existence of a letter Carr had written to the Notts Secretary, Captain H. A. Brown, at the start of the season, which begins: "This is the most awful team I have ever had, the batting is awful and the bowling, my god." Or perhaps they did. Larwood was not only unfit, Carr was worried that unless he was operated on, and for that he needed "the sanction of the MCC," the great bowler "will never bowl again." There would be much to say, Carr promised, at the forthcoming selection meeting, but speaking for himself, "I hope it rains for the rest of the season."

Carr was used to adversity. In 1926 he had captained England in the first four Tests against the touring

Australians, with no great distinction, it must be said. He was therefore dropped for the final match on the grounds that he was unfit, a claim he angrily denied. Carr despised Lord's attempt at diplomacy. He was fit enough, he told whoever would listen, but the selectors had chosen to turf him out. He did captain the Test team twice against the South Africans in Notts Championship year, but that was as far as international recognition went.

After his remarks about how he lost the England captaincy in 1926, Carr wasn't much favoured at Lord's. He was too much the individualist as well as very plainly a hard-drinking man. In 1930 the ridiculous Lady Astor asked a question in the Commons about whether England's lamentable performance against the touring Australians that summer might not have been due to their preference for alcohol to tea, tea being the reputed beverage which Armstrong, the Australian captain, required his men to swallow.

Lady Astor, it should be said, had a habit of asking such questions. Rather more than ten years later she enquired in the Commons whether the reversals in the Desert might not have been brought about by the visits of British troops to the brothels of Cairo, and in the summer of 1944 she was at it again, suggesting that able-bodied men were somehow dodging their duty. They were, she claimed, not prepared to join in the invasion of continental Europe. This was the same Lady Astor who before the war had been extolling the virtues of Adolf Hitler. Good to be able to report, therefore, that she was skewered by the poets Ian Fletcher (in his bawdy "Ballad of the Lady Astor") and Hamish Henderson, whose "Ballad of the D-Day

Dodgers", sung to the tune of Lily Marlene, is one of the most powerful laments for soldiers to come out of the second world war. Here are the last two stanzas:

> *Dear* Lady Astor, you think you know a lot,
> Standing on the platform and talking tommy-rot.
>   You, England's sweetheart and its pride,
>   We think your mouth's too bleeding wide –
> That's from your D-Day Dodgers – in far off Italy.
>
> Look around the mountains, in the mud and rain –
> You'll find the scattered crosses – (there's some which have
>   no name)
>   Heartbreak and toil and suffering gone,
>   The boys beneath them slumber on.
> Those are the D-Day Dodgers who'll stay in Italy.

In 1930 Lady Astor, presumably taking for granted that Carr was still captain of the England team, was as wide of the mark as she was of mouth when she complained about the side's drinking habits. It was simply that the Australians were the better team, though, as has been earlier noted, Chapman's captaincy was perceived to be of poor quality. Hence, the appointment of Jardine, and hence the consequences.

Carr was by general agreement a good captain, at least of the County team. And it was his steadfast loyalty to his Players that led to him being fingered as a rebel and therefore vulnerable to authority. This may well explain both contents and tone of the letter his team wrote on his behalf at the close of the 1933 season. The fervour of their hope that Carr will be spared "many years to continue as the county's captain" does rather suggest that they sense a coming crisis, one in which his rebellious instincts might well do him no favours.

"There had always been something of the 'rebel' in Carr's make-up," Wynne-Thomas says in his *History of Notts. CCC.* (p 181.) Knock away the quotation marks round the word rebel and you have the nub of the matter. Carr's loyalty to Larwood cost him the captaincy of Notts. For a full account of the events of 1933-4 which ended in his dismissal interested readers are referred to Duncan Hamilton. What follows is a summary, mainly drawn from Hamilton's biography, Peter Wynne-Thomas's *History*, Birley's *Social History of English Cricket,* and information collected during the writing of *The Trent Bridge Battery*.

According to the bare-bones account in *Who's Who of Cricketers,* the close of Carr's first-class career "was brought about by the arguments concerning 'bodyline' bowling. He was dismissed by the Notts Committee in December 1934, but forced an Extra-ordinary General Meeting of the County Club which demanded the sacking of the Committee and the reinstatement of Carr. Subtle manoeuvring however managed to reverse the decision of the Extra-ordinary Meeting of the Club's AGM and Carr was not seen again in County cricket." Like Jardine, Carr took himself off to a world of business and horse-racing. His father, a rich stockbroker whose original home was Rempstone Hall, between Nottingham and Loughborough, had moved to Yorkshire to be near the string of race-horses he had acquired, and Carr joined him there. The loss was therefore to cricket rather than to Carr's own interests.

His crime had been to give public backing to Larwood at a time when "Lol" was refusing to apologise for his bowling in the 1932-3 Ashes series, and this despite being asked –

"required" is hardly too strong a word – to do so by Lord's and by his County Committee. Not for nothing was Larwood a son of Sutton-in-Ashfield (actually the adjoining village of Nuncargate), birthplace of Billy Barnes and Tom Wass. In 1933, during a season when Larwood was anyway injured and as a result of which he played little, this refusal to apologise hadn't mattered. And perhaps, or so the authorities hoped, Lol's "stubbornness" would give way to "reason." But they were reckoning without their man.

In 1934 the Australians were once again in England for a Test series, Larwood was back playing, and although his fitness was not yet certain, so providing an excuse to omit him from the first Test which was played at Trent Bridge, he took five for 66 at Horsham against Sussex. He followed this up with six for 51 against Lancashire, a performance which would have been even better had the slips not dropped five catches off his bowling. These performances were enough for *The People* to insist that "Larwood must play" for England. But, the newspaper continued, "Carr, his county captain says, 'so far no invitation has been received by Larwood. When, and if, that invitation does arise, I can say that unless Larwood is allowed a free hand he will not play for England.' Jardine says the same. 'Larwood must play without bond or fetter if England is to win.'" In short, the great bowler wasn't going to be told by Lord's how he should bowl.

With Carr and Jardine supporting him, Larwood gave an exclusive interview to the *Sunday Dispatch* in which he said the he refused to play in any more Tests. "Politicians," he claimed, "are trying to hound me out of cricket. I was fit for the last Test, but they feared I would burst the Empire."

This may seem vainglorious but Larwood had reason for making the claim, one that was immediately dismissed in the following morning's headlines, reported by Wynne-Thomas. "Cabinet Ministers deny Larwood's allegations. Bowler's charge of political interference is 'Extraordinary Moonshine.'"

No, it wasn't. We can be certain of this because Carr passed on to Larwood a story he had heard on good authority. J.H. Thomas, Secretary of State for the Dominions and a man Hamilton rightly describes as "a canny, calculating, and efficient politician," had in private conversation let it be known that "No politics ever introduced in the British Empire have caused me so much trouble as body-line bowling."

Of course, Thomas didn't *mean* it, or so he said when challenged in public over the remark. But that is the way with "unattributed" remarks from politicians, or remarks that are let slip or dropped casually into the conversation and spoken with a knowing smile. Hamilton quotes the historian A.J.P. Taylor in his *English History 1914-1945,* who was convinced that Larwood "was dropped from future Test teams at the insistence of J. H. Thomas." Insistence is perhaps not quite the best word. Insinuation would better hit the mark. But one way or another there can be little doubt that Thomas wanted it understood that the continued omission of Larwood might be no bad thing.

This leads to the inevitable question: whose ear was Thomas bending? Who was privy to the insinuation? Which leads to a further question: whose was the good authority Carr relied on when telling Larwood that he was now perceived as a threat to Empire? The answer in both cases is, Sir Julian Cahn. Cahn was an immensely wealthy Nottingham-born businessman and philanthropist; he was also a would-be sportsman who used money to buy himself the best connections he could find, both off and on the sportsfield. He used money to become Master of the

Burton Hunt, in which capacity he was rumoured, with no doubt malicious intent, to spend rather more time falling off his horse than managing to keep upright on it.

But Cahn's real passion was for cricket. Here, his incompetence was probably unsurpassable. It was said, for example, that his slow bowling involved sending the ball so high that he had ample time to walk after the descending leather and catch it before it reached the batsman. He wore inflatable pads especially designed for his weak shins and which he had his chauffeur pump up for him while he dictated letters. The pads proved useful in persuading no-doubt compliant umpires that the ball ricocheting off them had in fact hit Cahn's bat, and the runs thus accrued could be set against his name.

At first blush Cahn seems an amiable eccentric, one of those men who litter the histories of sport with their innocent, entirely hopeless yearning for a prowess they can never achieve. Nothing could be further from the truth. At one time Basil Haynes and I contemplated writing his biography, but the more we talked to people who had known him the more difficult it became to find him a sympathetic character. He was not merely ruthless in his business dealings and his philandering, he took for granted that as a man of wealth he could bend people to his will; and he was quite ready to break them if they in any sense disobliged him. He wasn't a nice man.

Cahn owned two private cricket grounds. One was laid out at Stanford Hall, a mansion just outside the town of Loughborough. Cahn acquired the Hall in the late 1920s. In addition to its immaculately kept cricket field, there was a nine-hole golf course, a pool for performing seals, and a private theatre complete with Wurlitzer. There, Cahn gave displays of prestidigitation a good deal more competent than his attempts at batting. Moreover, he regularly entertained bits of royalty at Stanford Hall. I have seen a photograph of a visiting weekend party which included the Dukes of Gloucester, Norfolk and Kent, plus their wives, all of them making plain their distaste for the man off whose gold plate – hired for the occasion – they dined. Their smiles are fixed or they stare aloofly away from the camera. One or two gaze ahead with a kind of idle disdain. We may be in receipt of Cahn's hospitality, the looks say, we are graciously prepared to dine off the gold dinner service, but we are certainly not prepared to give the impression of feeling any gratitude for, let alone warmth toward, the man hosting the occasion. To study that group photograph is to be reminded of Dickens's description of those who gather round the dinner table of the brand-new people, the Veneerings, where "it is to be observed that all the diners are consistent in appearing to go to the Veneerings', not to dine with Mr and Mrs Veneering (which would seem to be the last thing on their minds), but to dine with one another." (*Our Mutual Friend*, Book 3, ch. 17.)

The air of near contempt the assembled nobility at the Cahns generates is easily explained. Cahn represented new money – trade. Even worse, he was a Jew. He wanted to ingratiate himself with the Establishment. The Establishment was quite ready to accept the hospitality his money bought, but they had no intention of accepting *him*.

Still, money bought Cahn the Presidency of Notts CCC. Before he became owner of Stanford Hall, money had brought him another cricket ground, this one within a stone's throw of Trent Bridge. It was at this immaculately kept ground with its rustic-style pavilion that Cahn received Larwood during the lunch-time break of a game being played in the early summer of 1934. Cahn had the previous year made much of his loyalty to Larwood, but he now revealed that he wanted him to apologise for bowling tactics which, it seemed, threatened his recall to Test cricket. Cahn had even prepared a letter for Larwood to sign. Addressed to the MCC, the typed letter both repented of Bodyline and vowed that it would not be repeated. All Larwood had to do was to sign on the dotted line. The letter would then be forwarded to Lord's and Larwood could expect his recall to the Test team.

Larwood refused. Alerted by Carr, he knew or anyway suspected that Cahn was acting at the MCC's request, and he also knew or suspected that the Secretary of State for the Dominions was behind the letter Cahn had prepared. This will explain Larwood's remark in *The Sunday Despatch* that politicians were trying to hound him out of the game. Cahn believed, so Hamilton suggests, that with Larwood's signature secured the MCC would grant him, Cahn, a seat at top table. But, Hamilton says, "the MCC thought differently...Well after Cahn's death in 1944, as demand for membership of the MCC was rising, the President of the club wrote to its Treasurer to caution him: 'If we apply too stringent an economic sanction, we will find the place full of Sir Julian Cahns.'" (*Harold Larwood*, p 212.) Nice to know that in post-war years anti-Semitism was still alive and well at the home of cricket.

But Cahn's plan and with them his hopes for his own acceptance at Lord's were scuppered when Larwood refused to sign the letter. He wasn't going to apologise for doing wrong when he believed he had done the right thing. He didn't see himself as a rebel, though he must have understood that circumstances were turning him into one. That he should have refused to sign the letter Cahn dictated comes as no surprise. In fact, he could hardly have done Cahn's bidding without lowering himself in his own and his supporters' eyes, among whom was Carr.

And Cahn? If *only* he had continued to take Larwood's side, as he had initially done when the bowler returned from Australia, if *only* he had accepted that he was as much an outsider as the great fast bowler, if *only* he had told the MCC he wouldn't do their dirty work for them. Wishes aren't horses. When, soon after the outbreak of war in 1939, Lord Haw-Haw (William Joyce) took to the German-controlled air waves – "Germany Calling" – to read out a list of prominent Jews in the UK the Nazis would be coming for once the invasion had been accomplished – an event which at that time people feared would be soon – Sir Julian Cahn's name featured high up on the list. Hearing of that, Cahn apparently went deathly pale and, his doctors believed, probably suffered a mild version of the heart attack which would in 1944 kill him.

* * *

So Larwood, the greatest fast bowler of his age, never played for England again. Cahn's hopes – admittedly vain – of becoming a powerful presence at the MCC went up in smoke. And by the end of the year Carr had been sacked from the captaincy of Notts. His rebelliousness as defender of Larwood proved too much for the pusillanimous County Committee. Besides, he had earlier in the season spoken up for Voce at a delicate moment, and in the final reckoning that must have counted against him. This episode, far less well-known than the Bodyline controversy though it belongs to it, deserves to be set out here. For it, too, features rebels as loyalists and vice versa.

Early in July, the touring Australians came to Trent Bridge to play Notts. Carr was *hors de combat*. He had suffered a slight heart attack in the previous match at Worcester and was under doctor's orders not to play for the rest of the season. Ben Lilley (1895-1950), wicket-keeper and decent middle-order batsman, captained the Notts team. At the end of the first day's play Australia had been dismissed for 237, and Voce, who according to Wynne-Thomas was "using leg-theory", took eight for 66. By this time, the team for the final Test at the Oval had been announced, and Voce was not included. His omission no doubt added venom to his bowling.

In their reply Notts scored 183 and then in came the Australians again. They had scored 3 runs without loss, and Voce had bowled two overs, when bad light stopped play. The next morning, when play was resumed, there was no sign of Voce. Where was he, the large crowd demanded to know. "After persistent enquires," Wynne-Thomas tells us, "the Secretary announced over the Tannoy that Voce was suffering from shin trouble and on medical advice would not take the field."

The crowd did not believe this. As a result, when the Australians declared at 230 for two, "a group gathered in front of the pavilion and booed." Carr, who was in the pavilion at the time, announced that if he had been captain Voce would have played. Wynne-Thomas says that "Rumours then circulated that several of the Notts Committee had resigned, but this was denied. Further rumours suggested that the Australians had objected to Lord's about Voce's bowling and pressure had been out on Notts to withdraw him from the final day's play." (pp 178-9.)

Wynne-Thomas declines to say whether the rumours had any basis in fact, though it seems certain that they did.

Birley notes that "The reverberations continued in Nottinghamshire, and after a match against Middlesex at Lord's – again with Carr absent, but vocal off-stage in support of his bowlers – more complaints were made and the committee once more apologised." Once more? This must mean that Birley takes for granted that the Australians had complained about Voce at Trent Bridge. As to the Middlesex complaint, Larwood was scathing. "Middlesex was also Plum Warner's club: he was one of the first to squeal." But then Warner had a knighthood to consider.

* * *

On December 22nd 1934, Notts Committee announced that Carr had been replaced as county captain by George Hearne and Stuart Rhodes. In between playing games of county cricket, these two young batsmen were regulars in Cahn's private team. It seems that he was in a position to shoehorn them into the joint captaincy, and his involvement in their promotion must be largely down to his rage at Carr's tipping the wink to Larwood about what lay behind the plan to get the bowler to sign the letter of apology prepared for him.

But the acceptance by the Committee of Cahn's move sufficiently incensed the members for an Extraordinary General Meeting to be called. About two and a half thousand people attended, among them the deputy Lord Mayor of Nottingham, H. Seely Whitby, who was bearing a signed statement from Bill Voce in which the bowler said that he had been fit to play on the final day of the game against the touring Australians. A long, bitterly acrimonious meeting ended with a vote of No Confidence. As a result the club Secretary, Dr Gauld, who had pronounced Voce unfit, resigned, and before long the entire Committee had tendered their resignations.

Matters then became even more complicated. Both Lancashire, who it will be remembered had a decade earlier got rid of Parkin, and Middlesex, under Warner, made public announcements to the effect that they would not play further matches against Notts if the county adhered to leg-side theory. There is no need to follow the ins and outs of what followed before order and a new County Committee – largely made up of the old Committee – was put in place. But the wreckage from the plan Jardine made in order to bring back the Ashes was considerable and wide-spread. It ended his own career as cricketer, and it ended the careers of Larwood and Carr. To repeat, their very loyalty to a cause turned them into rebels.

Meanwhile, Warner, adept as was said of someone else at nailing his colours to the weather vane, remained the voice of unctuous authority. In 1937 he was knighted for his services to cricket.

One last point deserves to be made. At about the moment Carr was being sacked, G.O. Allen took up his duties of captaining the touring MCC side in Australia. Presumably he had ensured that his party would include no perfect swine, let alone any gutless, uneducated miners. The visitors won the first two Tests. They then lost the last three and with them the series. In an odd way, Honours had been restored.

Allen captained the national side only once more. That was when in 1946 an MCC side toured the West Indies. They did not win a single match.

Chapter 11: Orders Restored

The rebellion of the lower orders – those uneducated miners – and of two maverick gentlemen, was effectively at an end by the beginning of the 1935 season. Whether Jardine and Carr had abandoned cricket or it had abandoned them is a moot point. What isn't in question is that with their going, MCC and Lord's once more exercised authority over who did what and, equally important, didn't. An edict was issued to umpires that they should disallow "persistent and systematic bowling of fast, short-pitched balls at the batsman standing clear of his wicket." Two cautions were to be given any offending bowler. If he nevertheless persisted in offending, he would be taken off and not allowed to bowl for the remainder of the innings.

Birley is surely right to say that the words about the batsman "standing clear of his wicket" constitute a strange proviso. What can they mean? Not crouching behind it? Not standing bang in front? Whatever, the upshot of the new regulation was, as many bowlers complained, likely to make cricket even more of a batsman's game. Another regulation to supplement the complicated Laws governing

LBW decisions was therefore introduced, according to which, if the batsman was hit on part of his body "on an imaginary line wicket to wicket, even if the ball pitched outside the off-stump," he could be given out LBW.

Larwood coped well enough with the new edicts. In 1936 he headed the first-class bowling averages, but two years later persistent injuries forced him out of the game. As for Voce, he took 139 wickets in the 1935 season, and in the 1936/7 tour of Australia he was England's best bowler, with 26 wickets at an average of 21.53. But neither he nor Larwood ever forgot nor forgave what they regarded as an act of betrayal by MCC and Lord's.

In the topsy-turvy world of that era's cricket, other one-time rebels of the 1932-3 tour turned loyalists and, as a result, prospered. Chief among them was Walter Hammond. At the conclusion of the tour Hammond had sung the praises of Larwood and Voce in wrecking the Australian batting. But once back in England, he began to dance to a different tune. Hammond says nothing about this in his own memoirs, but the likeliest explanation for his about-turn is that he wanted to change his cricketing status. Hammond (1903-1965) began his first-class career in the 1920s as a Player but in 1938 joined the Gentlemen, prompted by his awareness that "shamateurism" would allow him to recoup some of the money he had lost on unwise business ventures, and at the same time put him in line for the England captaincy. He at once succeeded in the latter objective though he did far less well on the business front. Birley calls him "chronically insecure", which seems a fair assessment of a man who appears never to have been at ease with himself except on the cricket field.

In some ways Hammond is reminiscent of Arthur Shrewsbury, although unlike Shrewsbury he didn't end up by taking his own life. But the two great batsmen were at one in their distrust of authority, their wish for financial security, their uneasy – not to say resentful – suspicion that the social status which would guarantee them unquestioning acceptance at Lord's might not be within their reach. Hammond apparently always dressed impeccably. There is a very odd passage in Neville Cardus's *Autobiography* (1947), in which he remarks that "The advent into cricket, and into the Yorkshire XI of all places, of a Herbert Sutcliffe was a sign of the times; the old order was not changing, it was going; the pole was fall'n; young boys and girls were level now with men; captains of cricket were henceforth called "skipper" by all self-respecting professionals, never 'Sir'. Our Sutcliffes and Hammonds, with their tailors in Savile Row, have taken us far beyond echo of Billy Barnes and his rough horny-handed company of paid cricketers of the eighties and nineties – savages born too soon to benefit from Mr. Arnold Forster's acts of Educations." (p 159.)

In so far as this makes any sense at all, it seems to be a lament for the good old days, when Players knew their place, and the Education Acts of 1870 hadn't put high-falutin' ideas into their knuckle-heads. Cardus's own high-falutin' misquotation from *Antony and Cleopatra* (it should be "the soldier's pole is fall'n") suggests that Hammond would have done cricket a favour by turning up to work, that is to cricket, in shabby jacket and trousers or – who knows – a Phrygian cap as indication that he was a manumitted slave, a beneficiary of Liberty, Equality, and Fraternity. But this of course would place him on the side of rebellion. Surely a Savile Row suit makes him one of the loyalists?

And so Hammond has been adjudged. Because, having earlier extolled the age when "cricket at Old Trafford was luxuriant with Maclaren (sic), Spooner and Tyldesley squandering runs opulently right and left", Cardus mourns the vanishing of the "romantic flourish" from cricket. "I even reacted against the romanticism in my own cricket writing. The lyric gush, the 'old flashing bat' and 'rippling green grass' metaphors gave way to, or became tinctured with, satire if not with open irony. Hammond no longer inspired me into comparison between him and the Elgin marbles; I saw something middle-class and respectable about his play, and was vastly amused and relieved when occasionally he fell off his pedestal and struck a ball with the oil-hole of his bat, or received a blow from a fast ball on his toe." (p 152.) Though both "old flashing bat" and "rippling green grass" are clichés, neither is a metaphor. And any comparison Cardus felt himself entitled to make between Hammond and the Elgin marbles indicates nothing so much as the paucity of his imagination. Not even the white of marble and a cricketer's whites have anything in common, and the athletic pose struck by one or two of the Greeks is entirely different from Hammond's cover drive.

As for Cardus's would-be lordly assessment of Hammond's play as "middle-class and respectable", it strikes me as nauseatingly sentimental, an unfocussed insistence on the "luxuriance" of those earlier days when the batsman Cardus persists in giving as Maclaren was apparently squandering runs right and left.

But there is more than sentiment at stake here. In calling Hammond middle-class Cardus must have somewhere in mind the great batsman's rather desperate search for status as a gentleman, one that anticipates Hutton's attempt to cultivate a standard middle-class manner of speech when he became England captain in 1953. It is a melancholy fact that Hammond's switch of status did him few favours. As he records in *Cricket's Secret History* (1952), "Apparently it is only the nominal status, not the man or his characteristics, to which exception is taken. I can say this because I captained England, after most of a cricket-lifetime as a professional. I was the same man as before, or perhaps I even had a slightly declining skill by that time. But because I changed my label all was well." (Quoted in Birley, *A Social History of Cricket* p 255.)

But all was not well. Nor was Hammond the amateur the same man as Hammond the professional. He couldn't be. By becoming captain he inevitably separated himself from the Players who, talent apart, had previously been his coequals. He had to enter the field of play by a different gate, he must often have been required to change in a different room of the pavilion; and on the score-card his name would now be printed as W.R. Hammond, rather than Hammond, W.R.

* * *

So Hammond becomes a kind of trusty, a poacher turned gamekeeper. But among a younger breed of batsmen a new spirit of derring-do was emerging. Even Cardus would have found some difficulty in denying that, if not swash-buckling, Denis Compton (1918 – 1997) could be thought of as someone who batted with what commentators would invariably describe as a cavalier disregard for the steady virtues identified with middle-class respectability. Compton, who emerged in the latter half of the 1930s, was a rebel by instinct, at least in his refusal to bat by the rules. Anyone wanting to put together a considered assessment of his genius – and as a batsman he was a genius, no doubt about it – inevitably made comparisons with those forerunners of the "Golden Age" of cricket, virtually all of them Gentlemen.

But Compton could also be seen as a man of the Thirties. Not the cliché-image, muffler-and-cap thirties, not the dogged, often down-at-heel thirties, though. For all that he was a Player, he was or anyway seemed a million miles away from drabness. Rather like Fred Astaire, whose charm, grace and insouciant deviltry are often said to have brought compensatory delights to the dark days of the Depression, so Compton, with his incredible fleetness of foot – he really did "dance" down the wicket to fast bowlers and often late-cut them – lit up English cricket with his boyish, lissom grace.

In *Cricket Prints,* Robertson-Glasgow, who saw Compton from the time he came into the Middlesex team in 1936, says that "Enjoyment, given and felt, is the chief thing about Compton's batting. It has an ease and freshness which the formality of the first-class game has not injured. It is … a breath of half-holiday among work-days." (p 113.) That's good, although it should be noted that like the even greater Garfield Sobers, Compton could play with classic correctness when that was required.

There were rumours, which did him no harm, that his good looks gave him a status among the ladies which suggested comparison not so much with Astaire as with Clark Gable. However exaggerated these rumours may have been, you certainly couldn't imagine Compton shuffling into line to pay his humble respects to his supposed betters. It seems fitting that a few months after he scored his first century for England, of 102, against Australia at Trent

Bridge in early June, 1938, Lord Hawke died. And though, as we shall see, the cricketing establishment Hawke did so much to bring about and keep in order didn't die with him, it was living on borrowed time.

* * *

Whether Hawke would have approved of Compton is doubtful. He could hardly have denied his genius, but he would almost certainly have frowned on his disregard for some of the proprieties by means of which Players kept to the due order of things. But Hawke would certainly have approved of the other great batsman who was beginning to show himself in the late 1930s, especially as Len Hutton was a Yorkshireman, whose 364 at the Oval in 1938 not only became the highest score ever made in a Test match, surpassing the 334 Bradman had made at Leeds in 1930, but also ensured that although Australia retained the Ashes, the series itself ended as a draw. (One victory each, two drawn, one abandoned.)

Post-war, Hutton would go on to lead England. And to his great credit, he resisted the suggestion from Lord's that he should turn amateur before they named him captain, a conversion which would have suited them no end and for which they no doubt offered him more than adequate remuneration. Hutton chose to remain a professional, a Player not a Gentleman. In 1957, Compton, his glory days gone, became an Amateur, a Gent. But he could never have captained England. With Bill Edrich, he did, it's true, captain his county for a couple of seasons in 1951 and again in 1952, and in 1950/1 was Vice-Captain of the MCC Australian tour, but without much distinction. He was too much the maverick, the individualist.

And a rebel? Yes and no. Compton certainly didn't lead the life of a sober-sides, early to bed and early to rise, forelock-tugging Player. He would have been contemptuous of older professionals, like Fred Root (1890-1954), the Derbyshire and then Worcestershire bowler who in the 1930s was himself contemptuous of all attempts to brighten up cricket. "Petty and puerile," Root called them. And this, though Robertson-Glasgow recalls Root as "endowed with contempt for adversity and all pettiness, [who] fought and toiled and joked through anything that batsman or climate could set against him." (*More Cricket Prints*, p 54.) Despite the occasion of George Gunn's fiftieth birthday, one which Gunn celebrated in typical style by scoring a century against Worcestershire, when Root refused his captain's request to take the ball for a second go at the great batsman – "I'm not bowling to that old bugger again," he reputedly said – Root seems the quintessence of the uncomplaining professional on which cricket between the war depended. Solid and stolid. You couldn't attach either of those terms to Compton.

And yet it might be said that Compton was nimble when it came to staying within bounds of the acceptable. For all his scapegrace airs, he wasn't a true rebel. He made more money from the game than most other Players of the age and as it was "new money" he certainly couldn't be counted among the Gentlemen. But he didn't need to be, any more than he needed to be among the echt rebels. "We shall want more Fred Roots in post-war cricket," Robertson-Glasgow ends his account of the toiler in sun and rain. *More Cricket Prints* was published in 1948. To discover just how prescient Robertson-Glasgow's words might be leads us to the next chapter.

Chapter 12: Spirit of the Age

Fred Titmus (1932 – 2011) began his career as a professional cricketer with Middlesex in 1949. Later, he recalled that although he had no clear memory of his first wage packet, he thought it amounted to £2.10s. (10 shillings old money equals the modern 50 pence.) But, he adds, "It would have been all the same if it had been thirty bob." For Titmus, as for many another talented young sportsman of his generation, life as a cricketer provided the quickest way out of Manchester. Such a life might not lead to fame and riches – and indeed most professional cricketers of any era could and can expect neither – but the compensations that playing cricket offered were enough for anyone aspiring to play cricket professionally to slam the door on a more conventional career. So, at least, most have always decided.

Such compensations may not at a glance seem obvious. To repeat an earlier observation, previous generations of sportsmen understandably preferred life in the open, however uncertain its promises, to one spent cooped up in factories or other forms of industrial labour. But after 1945, employment was not hard to come by, wages were comparatively good – miners, for example, averaged twice as much in weekly wages as the young Titmus earned – and conditions of work had greatly improved from what had typically been the case in pre-war England. Why then choose the insecure life of sport in preference to any of these things?

In an excellent essay on "The Players: An Examination of Professionalism in Cricket," John Arlott, writing in 1948, details the comparatively poor financial rewards the average county professional could expect to achieve. Wages for the professional cricketer in post-war England were never very high, even for players contracted to the wealthiest counties, and despite the fact at that time county grounds were full or any rate well attended for most games. "An established member of the Yorkshire team receives about £700 a year, out of which he must pay his match expenses," Arlott notes. But few counties could come near to matching that. "One county pays £22 for every 'four-day' match (Saturday, Monday and Tuesday, but involving Sunday) and £18 for every three-day match. (Wednesday, Thursday, Friday.) This applies whether the game be 'home' or 'out'; when 'out' the player is expected to pay his own expenses. Another county pays £12 for a four-day match, £10 for a three-day match, and £1 per day for expenses on 'out' matches."

Given that there were roughly twenty-six county games during a season, this meant that an average county player could expect to receive about £500 for his season's work. Some counties, Arlott adds, "grade" their players, the star players receiving £550, the lower-graded men £450. But take into account hotel or lodging-house bills, meals, laundry (heavy bills, these, because cricketers were expected to be impeccably turned out), travel, and it is at once obvious that hardly anyone could expect to make much money from being a cricketer.

There were exceptions, Cyril Washbrook's Testimonial brought in a record £14,000, and Denis Compton, "the Brylcreem Boy", was reported to pocket £1500 a year from advertising fees, sums both cricketers could perhaps put aside for the day when their careers had finished; but such bankable money would be beyond the average player. For as Arlott explains, even supposing that a county pro. escapes prolonged injury – which few do – and loss of form – and again few do – twenty years employment is about as long as he can reasonably anticipate. And then? He may find employment as a coach, he may be retained to do menial jobs around the county ground(s); he may even qualify to become an umpire. But by and large he can look forward to no job security, no pot of silver (most benefits brought in precious little, some none at all, and, anyway, the granting of a benefit was at the whim of the Committee and by no means guaranteed); and Arlott implies that in these and other respects matters may not have greatly improved since earlier days. At all events, he refers without comment to a *Series of Talks With Old Yorkshire Cricketers,* contributed "by 'Old Ebor' (A.W. Pullin) to the *Yorkshire Post* in 1897-8, in which it is revealed that, in Arlott's words, "many of the greatest Yorkshire players of the middle and early second half of the last century were then in a state of abject poverty bordering, in some cases, on starvation."

Do you really want to be a professional cricketer, seems almost to be the question hovering over Arlott's essay. And as though to drag this into the open, he adds that the player "has no trade union. He can be dismissed without reason on personal grounds. He can be denied a benefit which he has morally earned but which he has no right to claim. There is no guarantee of his security should he be ill or injured for any appreciable period beyond the end of his contract. He can draw crowds running into thousands and fill the headlines of the press of an empire and yet be living on less than the wages of a good artisan. His career is over before he is fifty and he must make his own provision for his subsequent years."

Why do it? Arlott's reply, as we might expect, is both measured and considerate. It comes in the last section of his essay, under the sub-title "The Romantic Pro.'" "The playing of county cricket," Arlott says, "is not a living, it is a life." And this life includes the camaraderie of fellow-cricketers, the allure of pitting yourself against others, and the attraction of possible fame. Such attraction, Arlott wryly notes, "has often not been resisted by philosophers of repute. Surely, then, the man who has taken delight in matching his limbs and brain against another's may be forgiven for preferring fame to the obscurity of a steady job in an office or factory."

There is more, much more to draw the young hopeful into the life of a professional cricketer, including the possibility of travel, either across the country or, in rare instances, to different cricket-playing nations; but in the end the decision to join the ranks of professional cricketers defies rational explanation. "On a sane and economic level no argument can be adduced for a man becoming a county cricketer," Arlott concludes: "he is valuable to the student of social history only as an example of the incurable romantic – but it is difficult indeed to deny him sympathy, perhaps even envy." (*Concerning Cricket,* 1949, pp 12-29 passim.)

This is a splendid essay, both in its unsentimental, coolly realistic assessment of what the life of a county professional for so long was, and beyond that in its sympathetic, *practical* understanding of the cricketer's vulnerability to the many external forces that may end a career. And in his balancing these against the compensatory rewards, often slight, sometimes almost invisible to the naked eye, Arlott entirely avoids the besetting sin of nostalgia which throws its misty light over so much writing about cricket. He neither glorifies the gentlemen amateurs, nor does he patronise professional cricketers, as is so often the case with writers from Cardus to Swanton; but his lively, sympathetic understanding of the reasons why young cricketers should choose to devote themselves to the professional game puts us in the way of recognising why, in the year that *Concerning Cricket* was published, Fred Titmus should opt for life as a professional crickter in preference to a career in a solicitor's office.

Re-reading Arlott's essay for the purposes of this book, and coming on his words about how it is difficult to deny sympathy, even a certain envy, for the county cricketer, I found myself remembering Vic Batt, a professional sportsman I'd met at the beginning of the 1960s. At that time I was living in Reading, and Elm Park, the football ground where Reading F.C. toiled in the lower depths of the old Third Division South being no more than a twenty-minute stroll away from the part of the town where my wife and I lived with our infant son, I'd frequently attend home matches. Among the Reading team, most of whom I can still recall, was a right-winger called Webb, inevitably known as Spider. Spider, who was short and squat, used to make frantic scurries up and down the touch-line, seemingly in possession of more arms and legs than nature intended, though they were rarely put to good use. Then, one Saturday, he was gone, and in his place was a rather better built wingman, who ran with some purpose along his line before nearing the corner flag, at which point he did as wingers were meant to do, hoofed the ball into the penalty area and watched as the inside forwards collided with various stationary objects – mostly comprised of the opposition's defenders – while the ball ran loose. After a few months, he, too, had gone.

But I saw him a season or two later on the cricket field. In July, 1964, the club I played for was involved in a full-day Saturday game against the Gentlemen of Berkshire, and after the game, which had ended in an amiable draw, I stood at the bar and said to the man beside me, one of the Gentlemen, "You're Vic Batt, aren't you?" He nodded. He was the winger who had replaced Spider Webb. "What happened?" I asked him, "you were pretty good. Did you simply stop playing football?" But no, he didn't look old enough. "Did you have to pack it in?" I was fairly sure that if he'd been transferred to another league club the news would have gone round Elm Park. But equally we would have heard of any injury that forced him out of the game.

No, he said, he hadn't been injured, not more than usual. He laughed as he said that. Then he explained. One Saturday he'd been sitting in Reading's changing room before a game while the then manager, Roy Bentley – former Chelsea and England centre forward – gave his usual pep talk. "He was going on about how Jonnie and Ray" – the full backs – "should take care as usual of the other team's wingers. 'Let them know you're there.' We all knew what he meant. Kick them round the ankles, get them in the back of the thigh with your knees, generally give them hell.' And I thought, yeh and the manager in the other changing room is saying the dead same thing.

'Well sod that for a game of soldiers.' I decided I'd had enough. So I left."

"You could do that?"

"I wouldn't have got another club, not in the league. But then I didn't want one. Took a job as a milk roundsman. Suits me fine." He now played semi-pro football for a team in the Southern League – "one evening's training a week and a fiver in your boot every Saturday" – and cricket all summer. He loved both games. As a teenager he had been on the ground staff at Lord's but didn't make the grade for Middlesex, and although one of the West Country counties were interested, he realised he hadn't got it in him to be a county player, so instead looked to football for his future. "But I'm glad to have what I've got. Steady job, as much sport as I want, and plenty of time for the wife and kiddies."

"I'm an all-rounder," he said of his cricket. "Bit of seam up and bat number five or six." He hadn't done anything much in the game we played, and although the Gentlemen of Berkshire were a good club and a fiver probably found its way into Vic's boots most Saturdays, he was a long way below Titmus's level. But he was, I'm pretty sure, a happy man. And he belongs in this narrative because Vic Batt was the kind of sportsman, for the most part uncomplaining, stoical, who never had to ask himself whether he enjoyed what he did. Vic only knew when he *wasn't* enjoying himself – which was when he was being kicked around the park by footballers doing as they were told. Choosing to get out of professional football along the route he took is hardly Rebellion Highway. It is difficult to make rebels out of such people as Vic Batt. Had he graduated to play for Middlesex or any other County, he might not have walked away from the county game, although we know that cricket continues to take its toll on marriages, so perhaps he would have done so.

In essentials Vic Batt, as with most professional cricketers of his era, was not a natural rebel. Yet most of them had to put up with a degree of condescension, not to say belittlement, that could have made rebels of them all, and did make rebels of some. The poet, Kit Wright, told me the following anecdote which illustrates the point. Apparently Roly Jenkins, Worcestershire's leg-break and googly bowler, who was also a decent lower-middle order batsman (he performed the "double" in 1949 and again in 1952), and played in a number of Tests for England, was on one occasion congratulated by R.E.S. Wyatt for an article that appeared under his name in a national newspaper. Wyatt, who had begun his gentlemanly playing days with Warwickshire, ended them with Worcestershire, for whom he turned out from 1946 until 1951. "Rather a good piece," he said in lordly fashion to Jenkins. "Who wrote it for you." "I wrote it myself," Jenkins said. "Who read it for you?"

Underlying Arlott's essay is a persistent question. Why do professional cricketers so often choose to accept the way they are treated. You have only to compare his approach with Cardus's sniffy protest, in an essay of 1952, that "the pressure of the spirit of the age hinders freedom and individuality," to understand what professional cricketers were up against in trying to make their modest living and to do so with honour and dignity. Cardus would have shown them all the door. "Life in the country is rationed," he goes on. "Can we blame Bloggs of Blankshire if in a four-hour innings he lets us know that his strokes are rationed." We may not blame him, is the clear implication, but cricket would be better off without him. Throw away the ration books, dismiss those who are playing for their careers – which means batting and bowling under orders. Bring back the golden age, bring back – oh, bring back MacLaren.

And in the Elysian fields of Cardus's imagination let MacLaren mix exclusively with the true Gentlemen of cricket. G.O. Allen, E.W. Swanton, later reported in his biography of that particular example, "mixed only with the *crème de la crème.*" Titmus would have been beneath his notice. This is not to say that either MacLaren or Allen would have behaved according to their hagiographers' expectations. But it is to say that as far as Cardus and Swanton, and those like them, are concerned, the gulf between Gentleman and Player, between cavalier disregard for prudential values and a mean, banausic care for them, is and remains impassable. If they noticed the likes of Vic Batt at all, it was only to glimpse them as objects too far beneath their dignity to require more than a cursory glance of approbation.

* * *

The Player has no trade union, Arlott says. Not only that. As after the first world war, when the old order was trying to insist that nothing had changed, and there was still a cult of leather arm-chairs, monogamy and briar pipes, to use the terms by which Orwell characterised the traditionalists' view of the 1920s, so in the 1940s the cricket Establishment was doing its damnedest to hang on to a world where Gentleman and Players could be regarded as virtually different species, though each was essential if cricket was to survive.

To take an instructive instance of this. In 1957, on the MCC tour of Australia, the manager, "Freddie" Brown (1910 – 1991), who in 1950/1 had captained the touring side in silk shirt, cravat, and with an entire lack of distinction, apparently "sought to restore something of feudal discipline, for example by his insistence that the professionals should not refer to his assistant, E.D.R. Eager, as 'Desmond' but as 'Mr Eager', and had aroused indignation by laying down paternalistic drinking rules." (Birley, pp 290-1)

As captain of Northants. Brown's *droit de seigniorial* ways went even further. He insisted, as though it was his God-given right, on making first use of the after-the-play bath; and as there was only the one tub in the Northants. pavilion, the rest of the team had to wait until he was finished, by which time the water was as scummy as it was cold. Meanwhile, "Freddie" was getting stuck into a large gin and tonic.

Anyone of a certain age will surely remember and be able to cite examples of the increasingly absurd efforts of the old guard to defend the supremacy of Amateurism in the period running up to the final abolition of the distinctions between Gentlemen and Players. "How can I live among this gentle/obsolescent breed of heroes, and not weep," Keith Douglas asked himself in "Aristocrats", one of the best poems to come out of the Second World War. Weep with laughter? Rage? Pity? All of these, no doubt. But at least those who went to war and were prepared to die did behave with a kind of cavalier, selfless heroism. The same can hardly be said for the wrinkled mastodons who clung to power at Lord's in the period between 1945-1963.

Which brings us to the question which now needs to be asked. Even allowing for the habitual stoicism of most professional cricketers, their wry acceptance of the lot they had embraced, why, in the post-war years, was there so little by way of protest against the order of things. One answer is, of course, that they had willingly agreed to become professional cricketers. Nobody forced them to do so. There was, after all, a world of work elsewhere. Another is, that, as Arlott, points out, there was no cricketing trade union. Then again, and as he implies, the kind of person who chose to become a county pro. was an incurable romantic. The phrase may seem vague, perhaps evasive, but it at least has the merit of identifying what so distinguished a social historian as Eric Hobsbawm called a deep-rooted conservatism about many Englishmen, a habit of mind that goes with a shrug, a shake of the head, and a mildly baffled, even irritated, but resigned acceptance of the way things are.

Such acceptance was I suspect taken for granted by those who saw themselves less as the appointed than as the natural authority in all cricketing matters. But year by year their grip was being loosened. Rebellion, however slowly it seemed to be in coming, was in fact on the way.

Chapter 13: Craft and its Values

And yet in the immediate aftermath of 1945, sport of all kinds seemed not merely to provide business as usual, but to operate as a thriving and reassuring constituent of daily existence. This must have had some part to play in prompting Fred Titmus to opt for the life of a professional cricketer. From our vantage point in the early twenty-first century, it is difficult, if not impossible, to appreciate the extent to which, in the years immediately following the end of war, sportsmen – and, just occasionally, sportswomen – became, in the cliché of the time, household names. And this applied to more or less all sports, including ones which have now become virtually extinct or enjoyed by a tiny minority compared to the thousands who then identified with them. The successes and failures of boxers such as Freddie Mills, Bruce Woodcock and Randolph Turpin, of cycling's Reg Harris, Victor Barna of table-tennis, of Geoff Duke, whose motor-cycling skills and daring guaranteed his repeated victories in the Isle of Man's T.T. race, of Joe Davies at the snooker and billiard table, of champion jockey Gordon Richards, were between them followed by millions. And these are only a few of the names that achieved prominence in the period we are now considering.

Despite the crowded arenas, stadia, race-tracks (for athletics, horse and dog racing, and motor cycling) and sports halls – and in the immediate post-war years the crowds were huge – by no means all of those who knew about these sporting heroes actually saw them in action. And if they did so, that was often courtesy of film clips in cinemas showing, at interval time, either *Pathé* or *British Gaumont* News. Failing that, they heard about them on the radio or read about them in the newspapers. And nearly everyone read newspapers, just as nearly everyone listened to the wireless. Between them, the two mediums, backed by cinema newsreels, broadcast not merely reports on, but photographic images of, those who rode to victory, went down to defeat, fought honourable draws. Names had faces.

Nothing new in that, of course. The nineteenth century had been rich in sporting prints, newspaper photography took off in the early twentieth-century, and cigarette cards featuring footballers and cricketers, a phenomenon especially of the inter-war years, were eagerly and widely collected, often by those too young to smoke but anxious to possess full teams of players and prepared to indulge in playground bargaining.

As for radio commentators and journalists: they were inevitably important in establishing the credentials of the individuals and teams about whom they spoke and wrote. They, too, became, if not celebrities, then recognisable and trusted names. Men and boys crowded round the wireless to listen to the various forms of Sports Reports, especially the Saturday afternoon football results. They switched on for Eamonn Andrews' or Raymond Glendenning's near-hysterical ringside commentaries on boxing contests, with "inter-round summaries" by Barrington Dalby, and sat up for the early hours' accounts of how British fighters coped with American opponents. (Badly, for the most part: I have never forgotten the voice of Rocky Marciano telling British listeners that "You sure have a fighter in Mr Don Cockell. I kept hitting him and he would not go down.") They bought favoured newspapers not merely to read about how the team they supported had got on in an important match, but to find out what Charles Buchan, Geoffrey Green, Peter Wilson, or some other "star reporter", had to say about the performances of other sides. The messenger became at least part of the message, which was that Sport Mattered.

In his essay, "So Over to the Cricket At ..." John Arlott speculates on how a cricket commentator can best put into words the apparent inaction during a passage of play in which few runs are scored, how to communicate "the sultry heaviness of the air, the steadiness of the batting, the grim relentlessness of the bowling. Shall he do it by bald, blunt statement, which must prepare his listener for minute after minute of *numerically* dull play? Or can he show the true nature of this tug-of-war – the tightness of the bowling and fielding, the grim, experienced, technically perfect batting of Hutton and Washbrook?"

Arlott's essay, which ought to be studied by all aspiring commentators, provides telling insights into his knowledge of the game's mechanics as well as his considered sympathy with cricket and cricketers, and in doing so shows why he was such a great communicator. It also shows his warm feeling for those who would never be stars. In the immediate post-war period, cricket commentary might come from county grounds far from Test match thrills.

Arlott imagines one such ground, where a middle-of-the-table game is heading for a draw watched by "a handful of spectators – old men too tired to go home – or with no home to go to – and small boys, to whom all cricketers are gods and their actions memorable." Add then two batsmen, steady if uninspired, and a bowler "who has sighed these many years for relief from doubling the parts of spearhead and solid body in his county's attack," and who bowls steadily, just short of a length, at the steady batsmen. But then, "some slight gust of wind, some wicket-keeper (with the neatness of Haydn Davies if the commentator's luck is out) suddenly interrupts the mild, restful afternoon which will know no headlines tomorrow .... With the minutest movement of the hand which holds the ball he removes one bail and looks enquiringly at the umpire. And the batsman is out – just as the commentator's voice has taken on the uneventful lull of the afternoon. Explanation is not easy." (*Concerning Cricket*, pp 82-4.)

Perhaps not, but what makes Arlott's essay especially cherishable is his awareness that, ordinary as the activity on which he reports may be, it merits his full attention, and that words have to be found that are adequate to it. The BBC commentator has a dual responsibility: to the cricketers on whom he comments and to the listeners with whom he communicates. And these responsibilities are of equal importance. He may, Arlott says, want to try to communicate at length something of the atmosphere of the ground from which he is reporting, but he cannot say these things, "lest they should prevent me from stating the precise score, which Mr. Smith, who has just dashed panting into his sitting-room to switch on his set, is so anxious to hear." These words should be printed in large type at the head of contracts for all those present-day Test Match Special commentators who witter on for hours at a time about sea-gulls, pigeons, buses, chocolate cakes and their companions' attire, without *once* telling the listener what the score is or even who is bowling.

Arlott is the ideal commentator, and not merely because he is solicitous of his listener's need to know the state of the match on which he is reporting. He is also solicitous of the cricketers themselves. Here, grandiose language is beside the point. The kind of lacquered romanticism in which so many commentators of an earlier time coated their subject does a disservice to the unobtrusive skills Arlott praises. For him, the average county cricketer is above all a craftsman. This comes out in his essay "The Craft So Long to Learn", where he suggests that the cricketer of southern England "plays cricket like the thoughtful country craftsman that he is." Arlott doesn't bother to identify his adaptation of Chaucer's original "The life so short, the art so long to lerne", though he probably enjoyed and hoped others would enjoy the allusion. He has no interest in parading his considerable knowledge of poetry, but his affirmation of the cricketer as craftsman, modest though it may seem, takes genuine and uncondescending pleasure in the craftsman's accomplishments. The kind of cricketer for whom Arlott speaks up "has not always been a Test Match player, perhaps he lacks the final combative spark of the northern cricketers, the extra dash of the gentleman of the London Fancy, but he has a warm quality of his own." (*Concerning Cricket,* p 9.)

If there is a touch of romanticism in this, it certainly doesn't tend toward the making of heroes into gods. Arlott's county cricketer is Mr Goodman Average. But –

and this is the crucial point – not only does the very ordinariness Arlott celebrates invite our respect, it establishes the labourer as worthy of his hire.

And there is a further point. Many professional cricketers in the period Arlott is talking about had fought in the Second-World War, just as a previous generation had fought in the first. Some, including such outstanding performers as Hedley Verity and Ken Farnes, died in it. A good number of those who returned to cricket had been exposed to suffering and hardship. Many were contemptuous of the officer-class which they saw as perpetuating a way of life they weren't any longer prepared to tolerate. The size of the Labour victory in July, 1945, was after all greatly boosted by the votes of serving men and women. "When I was demobbed," the comedian Harry Secombe later recalled, "I vowed I'd never again call anyone 'sir'". His words would have been echoed by sportsmen combatants.

This is the therefore context in which to understand what, slowly but inevitably, was to happen to cricket. The age of unquestioning deference was past. Time to begin a new.

* * *

Not that everyone saw matters in this way. Football also had its antediluvian specimens. Having scored two goals in England's great victory over Europe at Hampden Park, Wilf Mannion, Middlesbrough's inside-forward and by common agreement a player touched by genius, had to travel back to his native city in the corridor of a crowded third-class compartment while the FA big-wigs soaked up whisky in a first-class coach. And those of a certain age will remember how Bob Lord, chairman of Burnley

Football Club, master butcher and a man whose opinions on most matters make Dickens's Bounderby seem a model of Enlightenment, week after week took it on himself to assure the host of BBC Sports Report that professional footballers were quite content with the maximum wage and that if they weren't they knew what they could do. "Ah, he's a character, is Bob," the host would chortle after yet another of Lord's rasping denunciations of footballers who threatened to get above themselves.

Nobody representing the headquarters of cricket spoke like Lord. But many, perhaps most, thought like him. Professional cricketers – the Players – were, like their footballing counterparts, expected to toe whichever line was drawn for them. Questioning the wisdom of those in control or the fairness of how they, themselves, were treated, was not to be tolerated. To be sure, footballers were in some, perhaps most, respects even worse treated than cricketers. Gary Imlach's *My Father and Other Working-Class Football Heroes* (2005) provides gut-wrenching stories about the way Stuart Imlach, a highly-talented wing forward, was bought and sold by the clubs for whom he played as though he was of no more account than a piece of furniture. Imlach and others like him were moved from pillar to post, their families uprooted from one town and simply dumped in another as the selling and buying clubs dictated. And their sporting lives could end with abrupt suddenness, injury force a retirement which brought with it little or no chance of compensation. They were, all of them, subject to the system under which clubs retained or disposed of them under contracts they had no alternative but to sign and by which they were, as Gary Imlach says, shackled.

Reading about the treatment handed out to Stuart Imlach brings to mind Falstaff's brutal dismissiveness of the wounded soldiers he has pressed into service and who, he complacently reports, "are for the town's end, to beg during life." A fall into penury was by no means uncommon for professional footballers after their playing days were over. Increasingly, the footballers complained about this. Their especial bitterness was directed at the contractual system under which clubs had the right to buy and sell as they chose.

The protests against this eventually led to a successful challenge to the system. In 1960, the Newcastle player, George Eastham, asked to leave the club once his contract ran out. Arsenal, he knew, wanted to sign him. Newcastle said no. According to Garry Imlach, "A Newcastle director boasted that he'd see Eastham shovel coal rather than let him leave the club. But Eastham did leave. He walked out in the summer of 1960 once his contract had expired, took a job as a salesman with a friend who ran a business in Surrey and waited." In the figure of Eastham, Imlach says, the Professional Footballers Association "had the perfect candidate for a challenge to the retain-and-transfer system." (p 151.)

County cricketers had the opposite problem from the one that constrained and often humiliated professional footballers. The latter were moved at the whim of a club's directors. They might be loyal to the club by which they were signed, but the club saw no reason to be loyal to them. In contrast, cricketers were, with rare exceptions, tied to the one county for the length of their playing lives. They *couldn't* move. They had therefore no alternative but to accept whatever their county wanted of them. In his study of *The Precariat: The New Dangerous Class* (2011), Guy Standing makes a distinction between employment security

149

– having a long-term contract with a company – and job-security. An employee's salary may be safe, but not the actual job. The company is free to move employees from work they like doing, and for which they are trained, to work they dislike and for which they have no great aptitude.

When Tom Graveney asked to leave Gloucestershire it was because his job security had been taken away from him. He had been deposed as captain by an amateur he knew to be in all senses his cricketing inferior. His request was made a year after George Eastham asked to leave Newcastle – the consequences of which included the collapse of the clubs' contractual hold over Players, the end of the maximum wage, and a whole new era for footballers.

* * *

Cricket's authorities held on rather longer to a power which was, of course, based on the assumption that only Gentlemen knew how to safeguard the game's best interests. When a professional, Len Hutton, was chosen as captain of England to lead the side against the 1953 touring Australians, his few on-air remarks suggested that he had either been given elocution lessons or somehow learnt a strangulated way of making clipped utterances that sounded as woefully inauthentic as John Mills or Richard Attenborough speaking what might be termed Pinewood Cockney. That a great cricketer should have felt himself required to toe the line to Establishment-speak provides a sharp reminder of how rancid with outmoded notions of cricket-and-gentlemanliness MCC still was.

Birley tells us that when Hutton was appointed it was made clear to him that as a professional he was a stop-gap. "Trailing clouds of pre-war subservience, he inevitably felt at a disadvantage when dealing with illustrious amateurs in the committee room and over-anxious about the impression he made." (p 283.) Still, Hutton refused the suggestion he might like to change his status to that of amateur.

A rebel, then? No, not really. In the way he spoke and the words he used, Hutton seemed to accept his role as menial. Nevertheless, it was no doubt a great relief to Lord's when he could be replaced by the amateur, P.B.H. May (1929-1994). May, undoubtedly a great batsman, was also a stiff-necked and unimaginative captain, and it may be no coincidence that in 1956, the year after he became captain of England, his county colleague, Alec Bedser, wrote a long letter to the MCC's president, complaining that amateurs were taking the "plums" away from professionals, lending their names to advertising matter, and receiving salaries for employment as "secretaries" to county clubs and the like. The "Shamateurism" outlined in an earlier chapter, which had become institutionalised during the latter half of the nineteenth century, was still alive in post-1945 England, though clearly all was not well, not if a loyal and dyed-in-the-wool conservative like Bedser could find it in himself to protest against what he rightly saw as a form of protectionism, one which disadvantaged the professional cricketer. It is therefore not merely ironic but deeply instructive that, as we have already seen, more than a decade later, when Bedser was Chairman of the Selectors, he should choose to behave so brutishly to Tom Graveney. It was Bedser who as much as anyone was responsible for ending Graveney's career as a Test cricketer. A perfect example, it might be thought, of poacher turned gamekeeper.

Bedser's behaviour in 1969 confirms that by no stretch of the imagination could he be thought a natural rebel. Nor could the term be applied to that great bowler, Brian

Statham (1930 – 2000). Statham, as his nick-name "George" suggests, was the quintessence of reliability, of devotion to duty. He took fewer Test wickets than Trueman – 263 in 70 Test matches compared to Fiery Fred's 307 from 67 Tests – but this is commonly agreed to be because he was so accurate, so unyielding a bowler, that batsmen, relieved to be away from his daunting line and length, played more freely at Trueman and paid the price for rash strokes they had no opportunity to display against his opposite number. "They miss, I hit," was Statham's motto, and on his tours to the West Indies in 1953/4, then to Australia in 1954/5, when he was partnered by Frank Tyson, he performed outstandingly, as he did again in 1958/9, when he achieved better figures than either Tyson or Trueman. Mr Reliable, as he was sometimes known, Statham never let either Lancashire or England down.

So on the ship taking the tour party to the 1962/3 Ashes series he was understandably miffed when his captain, Ted Dexter, proposed to introduce regular keep-fit sessions that would be undertaken each morning before breakfast. Everyone was expected to join in. That, anyway, was the idea. But Statham was having none of it. Thanks, but no thanks, he told Dexter. His morning ritual would be what it always had been. A cigarette and a cup of tea. No more was heard of the keep-fit sessions.

Set Bedser and Statham's names beside those of earlier rebels considered in this book, and it confirms the impression that bowlers are to the fore when it comes to resisting authority. Their rebelliousness may not amount to much more than a show of mild truculence, but underneath the sometimes comic show there may well be, and often is, a genuine element of protest against the heavy hand of those who want to use it to press down on the infantry. Thus far and no further. Some years after Statham made his stand against what he saw as Dexter's modish health-and-fitness regimen, Nottingham's Barry Stead (1939-1980), staged a rather similar one-man rebellion when he and others were ordered back to Trent Bridge well before the start of the season. There was to be a general toning up of bodies and sharpening of reflexes so that for the first match the side could hit the ground running. This cliché, which for a while had currency among the management of successive England Test sides, was derived from keep-fit army tactics, especially those associated with the S.A.S. It has more or less dropped out now and has been replaced by "the need to keep focussed."

But while most at Trent Bridge did their best to live up to S.A.S. routines, Stead conspicuously failed to do so. He arrived back from Transvaal two days before the start of a season during which he bowled with all of his customary verve, his action as always that a clockwork toy whose spring has been wound super tight.

As for Trueman, his truculence was perhaps less that of the true rebel than of an almost parodic vaingloriousness, a posture intended to prove to the world that he was a fearless, no-nonsense "Tyke." It is commonplace to speak of Trueman's "boisterously know-it-all demeanour," and in his biography of a man who was certainly an outstanding bowler, John Arlott provides a vivid description of Trueman doing what he did best, bowl fast. "Body thrown forward, he moved first at a steady pad and gradually accelerated, hair flopping, and swept into the delivery process ... Trueman's body swung round so completely that the batsman saw his left shoulder blade: the broad left foot was, for an infinitesimal period of time, poised to hammer the ground … as the ball was fired down the pitch, his body was thrown hungrily after it, the right toe raking the ground closely beside the wicket as he swept on."

But Arlott doesn't shirk from commenting on Trueman's bull-headed contempt for anything and anybody he chose to believe was wrong, or his abusive attitude to some poor unfortunate who simply had the ill luck to be in his line of fire when he was delivering an ego-fuelled diatribe against authority, or someone who didn't share his often obtuse opinions on cricket, politics, personal relations or the universe. Rebelliousness of this kind is often no more than a fixed pose, a self-advertising and self-serving assertion of *non serviam.*

On at least one occasion, however, Trueman behaved with perhaps surprising and certainly tactful circumspection. Some time after Dexter retired from cricket, he either thought about standing for parliament in the Conservative interest or, more probably, was persuaded by a Tory pal to do so. Well, why not? Years earlier, the successful middle-distance runner and friend of Roger Banister, Chris Chataway, had entered the Commons and even gained a cabinet post as Conservative Minister of Posts and Telecommunications. Not everyone was impressed by this. There was an especially hilarious moment, shown on TV, when, as the minister emerged from a meeting at which he had addressed members of the TUC about a possible strike among post office workers, he was waylaid by union members. They were unhappy with the new employment terms they had been offered. Not only that. They didn't understand them. "What's this mean, Mr. Chataway?" one of them asked, thrusting into the Minister's face a piece of paper on which the

Government's proposal for a new pay agreement was set out. "Mutatis mutandis. What's that when it's at home?"

Chataway, who clearly hadn't a clue, waffled on about the phrase meaning something like a fair deal for all. Clearly, his expensive public-school education hadn't provided him with a working knowledge of Latin.

Nor, at a guess, had an expensive education greatly helped to develop Dexter's intellect. Great batsman though he undoubtedly was, he can't be said to have possessed much by way of political *nous*. Lack of judgement may be why he enquired whether Fiery Fred would be prepared to join him on the hustings of the South Wales constituency that Central Office, presumably tongue-in-cheek, had targeted for "Lord Ted." (The sitting MP was none other than Jim Callaghan.) On the other hand, the request may have contained a modicum of cunning, and not merely because Dexter must have known that Trueman would be far more likely to receive a sympathetic hearing from miners than he himself could anticipate. And if Dexter gained enough votes to at least disturb the composure of the politician whom journalists dubbed "Sunny Jim", that would be one in the eye for the Labour party.

Besides, Trueman owed Dexter. On a slow turner at Headingly in 1964, England were for much of the game having rather the better of the Test against the Australians. At one point, indeed, Titmus and Norman Gifford had reduced the tourists to 178 for seven. At which point Dexter chose to remove his spinners and bring Trueman and Flavell back into the attack. What followed was a series of would-be bouncers, from Trueman in particular, which, given the state of the wicket, amounted to not much more than long hops, and which were remorselessly hooked or pulled by Australia's no. six, Peter Burge. His onslaught eventually brought him a huge hundred and ruined England's chances of a victory that had been highly probable before Dexter's extraordinary intervention.

To his credit, Dexter admits in a chapter of his autobiography called "The Leeds Decision" that with hindsight he can certainly be accused of having made a bad mistake in not trusting his slow bowlers to finish off the Australian innings, although he then goes on to exonerate himself by remarking that, with the new ball due, most captains would have done as he did. This is, to say the least, unlikely. But then as Titmus wryly noted some years later, Dexter's captaincy took for granted the efficacy of Plan A. If for some reason that didn't succeed, there being no Plan B, the captain simply retired to the covers and practised his golf swing. It is entirely possible that inviting Trueman to Wales was as far as Dexter ever got with a Plan B for the realisation of his political ambitions. Sensibly enough, Trueman inspected his diary and found it to be entirely full with prior engagements for the period running up the election. He was therefore unavoidably absent when Dexter, mounted on a soap box, addressed some constituents he was attempting to convert to his cause. The great fast bowler did not therefore hear the advice offered his former captain by a miner who listened for some minutes in open-mouthed incredulity before offering Dexter some words of advice. "Go home, boy," he called out. "You're a joke."

After losing by some five thousand votes, which in fairness can be chalked up as a not discreditable achievement, Dexter took the miner's advice. No more politics for Ted. He turned to fiction and, with the aid of Clifford Makins, wrote a crime novel called *Testkill*. The novel is set during an Ashes series in England, in which the killer turns out to be a batsman described at one point as someone of "brilliance and beauty and strength", whose ability to face fast bowlers has been undermined by drink and drugs and, believe it or not, too much sex. Compton? No, the batsman-villain goes by the name of Byron. The great rebel of English poetry, who, it is piquant to reflect, tried to lose weight by wrapping himself in flannel, gripping a bat, and requiring his valet to bowl at him for hours at a time.

But as far as is known, Lord Byron never played an actual game of cricket. Whether Dexter intended to imply a causal link between rebelliousness and criminal activity is anyone's guess; but whoever – most likely Makins – named the villain Byron may at some level have intended to suggest such a link. Dexter was, after all, the quintessential man of the Establishment, one who seems never to have been much interested in the Players he captained or those whom he later helped select for England teams. It was Dexter who addressed Devon Malcolm as Malcolm Devon, and this at a time when Lord Ted was Chairman of Selectors of the England team in which Malcolm played.

* * *

It is poetic licence, perhaps, to imagine Byron's spirit transmuted into Colin Ingleby-Mackenzie, old Etonian and joyously irrepressible captain of Hampshire from 1958-1965, during which period his side won the County Championship and became famous for their deeds both on off the field. But he was a natural, unstoppable rebel against stuffed-shirt formality and the egg-and-bacon brigade. Lord of the Revels, if not of Misrule, when he was once asked whether he required his players to follow any regimen, Ingleby-Mackenzie memorably replied that he expected them to be in bed by 4 a.m of any match day. And on another occasion, when in the early hours he crashed his car into a shop-window in Reading and was as a consequence summonsed to appear before the beak on a charge of drunken-driving, most of his team-mates gave evidence to the effect that as on the evening in question he had drunk no more than several pints of beer and a bottle of wine, Ingleby-Mackenzie couldn't possibly be drunk, since everyone knew he could consume far more alcohol than that while remaining stone-cold sober. (This was of course before the introduction of drink-and-drive limits.)

Comparing him to Byron, Lord of Newstead Abbey, Notts., may be stretching it rather, though comparisons with that other man of Notts., A.W. Carr, are certainly in order. But unlike Carr, Ingleby-Mackenzie was not sacked.

Nor was Ingleby-Mackenzie's younger contemporary, Bob Barber (born 1935), who captained Warwickshire during the 1960s. That, and a public-school background, is however about all the two have in common. Barber was an excellent attacking left-hand opening batsman, and a good and able bowler (of the googly). But he had in his make-up far more of Freddie Brown than of the spirit of Hampshire's captain. Barber insisted on staying in a different hotel from that used by the Players, and in all ways he treated himself as apart from and above the rest. In this, he continued a line of Warwickshire captains, stretching back through Ron Maudsley (1918-1981), who for the season of 1948 jointly captained with the professional Tom Dollery, before dropping out of cricket for a number of years, after which he returned to supplant poor Dollery.

And before Maudsley there was Peter Cranmer, captain from 1938-1947. Not long before the Second-World War began, so legend has it, Warwickshire gave a trial to a promising fast bowler, who rebelled, or anyway protested, against Cranmer's decisions about when he should bowl, from which end and to what field. He was promptly given his marching orders. Rebellion in the pre-war Warwickshire ranks was not allowed, any more than, years later, it would be under Barber.

However, as will emerge later, the decision of the major batsman, Denis Amiss, to play for Kerry Packer, caused huge upset among the county's Players, amounting to near-rebellion. Such dissension would have been unthinkable in the years immediately following 1945. But then so would have been what caused it.

Chapter 14: Speaking Out of Turn

Trueman is one of several famous Yorkshire bowlers who, from Bobby Peel onward, have cast themselves in the role of rebel. Sometimes more sinned against than sinning, they have also gone out of their way to be bull-baited and badgered, as, with far more reason, Joe Gargery thought of himself as being. Among their number is Trueman's older contemporary, the left-arm spin bowler, John/Johnny Wardle. (1923-1985.)

Wardle was undoubtedly a great bowler. In his detailed and entertainingly informative account of spin bowlers, *Twirly Men* (2011), Amol Rajan has this to say about him. "Johnny Wardle … was the greatest exponent of slow left-arm orthodox and Chinemen bowling that ever played … He was one of the most effective of all bowlers at the defensive ploy of bowling a leg-stump line, from over the wicket, at the right-hander in the groove. Incapable of the zip off the wicket Verity achieved, and armed with fewer variations of flight than Rhodes or Bedi, he was nevertheless capable of spells of unplayable bowling, especially on sticky wickets. … His record at Test level, where he took 102 wickets [at an average of 20.39], bears out his dual capacity for attack and defence." (pp 228-231.)

One hundred and two wickets only, though. Plainly, something went wrong, but what exactly? The answer turns out to be, nearly everything, and not only because when Wardle was at his finest, Tony Lock, to the Yorkshireman's uncontained fury, was often chosen to play for England ahead of him. Lock, Wardle was by no means alone in saying, chucked his quicker ball. And he went further. The Surrey bowler's action was fundamentally suspicious, so Wardle believed.

Nor was it only Lock at whom Wardle pointed the finger. In *Spinner's Yarn*, Ian Peebles, recalling the MCC tour of Australia in 1954/5, notes that after the first Test, which Australia won at a canter, the tourists were certain that Australia's Ian Meckiff was a chucker, but "the [British] press was keenly aware that, in view of England's sad performance, any adverse comment on Meckiff would be regarded as a 'squeal', so were restrained in their comments. But when Meckiff cut loose at Melbourne and took six wickets for 38 runs in the second test, Johnny Wardle, writing in the *Melbourne Herald* ... denounced Meckiff in forthright terms as a 'chucker', and so set the atmosphere aflame." (p 193.)Given that Wardle was a member of the tourist party, it seems surprising that he was allowed the freedom of the press, although there is no surprise that, having been given it, he should be so unguarded in his comments. Speaking your mind was part of being a rebel, a Yorkshire rebel, a Yorkshire bowling rebel. And it was this which was eventually to cause the spinner so much trouble.

Wardle, who came from a mining family, began working life at the age of fifteen, apprenticed as a fitter at the Heckleton Main Colliery. Rajan tells us that two years later, as soon as he was seventeen, Wardle could have signed some sort of terms as a footballer for Wolverhampton Wanderers – presumably as an apprentice; but, he adds, "cricket paid better." Which, in Yorkshire was, as we have seen from John Arlott's essay on payment to cricketers in post-1945 England, the case. Few football clubs could, or anyway would, have equalled the £700 per annum Yorkshire paid its Professionals. Wardle must had thought he had made the right choice.

But as a cricketer he did not get off to a good start. He was in fact severely hampered by a bad coach – Rajan does not name him – who tried to make Wardle change his action, "getting him to cross his legs in the delivery stride." As a result, he completely and unsurprisingly lost his rhythm and with it his place in the Yorkshire side. It was only when he went back to his natural action that both rhythm and his team place returned. And soon enough he was earning a deserved reputation for being a bowler of outstanding gifts.

He was also becoming known for his short temper. Beware, the fielder who dropped a catch off his bowling. Beware, the batsman who edged a ball out of reach of a catch. Beware, even, the umpire who dared to turn down one of Wardle's appeals. And beware, above all, Yorkshire's amateur captain, Ronnie Burnet. In 1958 Burnet was appointed county captain at the age of 40. Wardle thought he himself should be captaining Yorkshire, that Burnet wasn't fit for the job, and he didn't keep such thoughts to himself. Soon enough, *The Daily Mail* published a series of articles in which Burnet's qualifications for the captaincy were held up for derision. It was an open secret that Wardle was the man behind them. Yorkshire Committee was not prepared to tolerate this display of disloyalty. Wardle was sacked.

In an unusually candid and often revealing autobiography, *Ball of Fire* (1976), Trueman writes with what feels like genuine sadness about the episode. He begins by acknowledging that for all Burnet's limitations as a cricketer, the new captain, who had for some years skippered the Second X1 before moving up to take charge of the County team, was "a natural leader." And he gives as an example of this Burnet's asking Brian Close on one occasion to open the batting and, when Close demurred, telling him "either go in first or go back home." (p 68.) But Trueman acknowledges that the appointment of Burnet rankled with Wardle. "I'm sure Johnny thought the job was bound to be his, because of his experience, knowledge and length of service, and he would probably have made a good captain, although I considered he had too severe an attitude to the younger players and expected too much from them too soon... In my opinion Johnny was the finest slow left arm bowler of my time, but he was denied a regular place in the Test side. Poor Johnny must have thought he was missing out on everything."

Trueman goes on to say that when Burnet took over, the atmosphere in the Yorkshire dressing-room was, in his words, "a bit tense," which made life difficult for Trueman himself, because he was, he explains, friendly with both Burnet and Wardle. But when the articles appeared in the *Daily Mail* it was obvious that a crisis point had been reached. At the moment of revelation, Yorkshire were about to begin a county match at Old Trafford. "Ronnie marched in," Trueman says, "shut the door and said: 'Right, lads, you may read some articles in the paper written by Johnny Wardle which will probably bring the other press lads and the radio people round here later today. You are to keep your mouths shut. As for Johnny Wardle, I've just sent him packing. He's finished with Yorkshire for good!"

And that, as far as the County was concerned, was that. But looking back, Trueman adds that he thought it "a great shame for such a magnificent cricketer to go out in public disgrace." He is also scathing about the later hounding of his friend. It wasn't necessary, he says, for Yorkshire "to be so vindictive when Johnny looked round for another job. They warned off other counties and he wound up playing on Saturdays in the Lancashire league." (pp 67-70.)

A similar if rather less intense vindictiveness was, as has been noted at the beginning of this book, directed at Tom Graveney, when a year or so later he objected to an amateur captain being appointed in his place, though in fairness to Burnet it should perhaps be said that he must have been a far superior captain to the amateur who replaced Graveney. At all events, in 1959 Yorkshire won the Championship under his captaincy. After that, he retired.

* * *

That same year, 1959, Surrey's Jim Laker, one of the finest spin bowlers of the modern era, also retired. If this seems mere coincidence, we should note that he, too, was soon to find himself ostracised by the cricketing establishment. Something was in the air. In Laker's case, ostracism resulted from his memoir, *Over to Me,* which was published in 1960. The *Who's Who of Cricketers* remarks in anodyne fashion that the book "caused some ill feeling." This is to put it very mildly. Birley is rather more to the point when he says that *Over to Me* "got Laker

banned from the pavilions of both the Oval and Lord's."
He had dared to criticise Peter May and the "high-handed
manner of F.R. Brown" when Brown had managed the
touring party to Australia. Laker, Birley thinks, "was
tempted into indiscretion by the lure of the sensationalist
trend – and by the hypocrisy that still festooned the game."

But Laker had good cause to feel aggrieved. He was
after all a great bowler and it is understandable that he
resented May, Surrey and England's captain, dictating
and/or interfering with his field placings, or telling him
how to bowl at particular batsmen, whether at Test or
County level. Moreover, like so many Players of his
generation, Laker was angered by the insistence on the
distinctions still maintained between amateur and
professional cricketers. On the Australian tour, Birley says,
"The professionals wryly accepted that the amateurs should
now get not only expenses but compensation for loss of
earnings. They had been startled on the voyage out,
however, by the rumour that this compensation was to be
tax-free, like their expenses. Laker commented that he had
seriously thought of turning amateur, adding sardonically
'I might have been better off.'"

To crown it all, in the same week that May won £500
from an Australian newspaper for scoring a century
between lunch and tea, "it was announced that he had
turned himself into a limited company." (pp 290-1.)
Shamateurism was alive and well, although there is no
reason to suppose that all Gentlemen skippers took
questionable financial advantage of their position.
Trueman, for example, observes that Ronnie Burnet was
an honest amateur "who only claimed his genuine
expenses." But that Trueman should think it worthwhile
commending Burnet for his honesty indicates clearly

enough that the majority of "amateurs" had no scruples about trousering whatever money they could lay their hands on.

Rajan inevitably has to take note of the bad feeling caused by *Over to Me*, but though neutral about the fact that soon after the book was published Laker was stripped of both his honorary memberships of Surrey and MCC, he does remark that Laker was something of a loner "and stubbornly introverted." He doesn't, praise be, try to provide a cheap psychological explanation for this nor to trace the introversion to Laker's roots. Instead he notes without comment the circumstances of Laker's birth and upbringing.

"Gentleman Jim", as Laker was sometimes, half-ironically known, was born in Shipley, near Bradford, in 1922. A Yorkshireman, he was a year older than Wardle, whom he would consider produced the finest spell of spin bowling he ever saw in a Test match, against South Africa on the 1957/8 tour, an opinion which, as Rajan says, "coming from the man who just months earlier had taken nineteen Australian wickets at Old Trafford in the greatest bowling performance cricket has known … has some clout." (p 229.) A mere two years old when his father left, he was the one boy among five children, and, like the others, born illegitimately. (Though this was still common enough among working-class families.) His mother apparently doted on him and he on her.

Like so many of his contemporaries, Laker fought in the second world war, came home to find that his adored mother was dead, and, while working at Catford for the War Office, "soon made it to Surrey, but not before he had enquired whether he might get into the Yorkshire side. Failure to do so, and the rejection he felt, led to his briefly returning to a career in the bank." Before the war Laker had worked for Barclays in Bradford and back he went, though not for long. Surrey called him, and he answered the call. So Rajan tells us.

Once installed at the Oval, the off-spinner began to thrive. Nevertheless, like Wardle, Laker was under-used by England, and it is impossible not to sense that, despite his deceptively mild manner – in later life his TV commentaries were positively soporific – he resented the comparatively few chances he had as a Test cricketer, and also the ways of MCC and Lord's. Peter May reportedly said that the very idea of Laker ever showing enthusiasm was absurd. But emotions can be disguised, and beneath those apparently immobile features, that unrufflable surface, deep feelings undoubtedly ran, understandably so. Yet having said this, it should be added that from the standpoint of the early twenty-first century, it is difficult to see why *Over to Me* caused such near-apoplexy among those whom Laker criticised.

Unless, that is, we accept that those lordlings, including the ineffable F.R. Brown, regarded themselves as above criticism, as they almost certainly did. The late nineteen fifties were still – just – a time when the distinctions between those who governed the game of cricket and those who were governed continued to baffle, reassure, or, of course, infuriate. Hence, that wondrous, infamous occasion when, as Fred Titmus walked out to bat at Lord's, a voice over the loudspeaker intoned a scorecard correction for the spectators' benefit: "For F.J. Titmus read Titmus F.J." Only Gentlemen could be allotted initials before their surnames. Only Gentlemen could be allowed to enter and exit the field of play through gates held open by white-coated attendants. For players, initials trailed behind.

But soon this would all change, and when the change came rebellion took on a markedly different appearance from that which the game was used to. It was no longer left to individual cricketers. And as TV helped to fund football to an unprecedented extent and in the process cut off the leg-irons of maximum-wage, retain-and-transfer contracts, so TV, or anyway the Australian channel owned by a rich entrepeneur, gave cricketers a chance to kick away the constraints which for so long had chafed their playing lives.

* * *

Before closing the present chapter it seems appropriate to devote a paragraph or two to the question of whether Wardle and Laker were produced by the times or whether they were natural, born rebels. Thirty years prior to Wardle's sacking by Yorkshire, Cecil Parkin had been dismissed by Lancashire. He had done no more than criticise the choice of Gilligan as England captain. Wardle, on the other hand, savaged his own County's choice of Burnet over him. His case is more like Graveney's, although from what Trueman says we can infer that Yorkshire hounded Wardle with a remorselessness that Gloucestershire CCC, for all their mean-mindedness, did not show towards Graveney. But in both cases, professional cricketers were proving openly hostile to County Committee decisions to continue with a policy of appointing amateur captains, and this can hardly be dissociated from the fact that they were operating in an age when the newly empowered Trades Unions not unreasonably caused their members to assume that "we are the masters now." And Wardle, like the Notts bowlers discussed earlier in this book, came from mining country, and had indeed begun work at a mine. This is not to argue simple cause and effect, but it is to say that from a young age he would have been familiar with the culture of mine workers, their political edge.

Warner and others of his generation would have thought Graveney and Wardle "Bolsheviks." And this was probably how the County Committees of both players regarded them, even if they didn't actually apply the term to either. But although the professionals' rebellion against authority could for the moment be contained, it seems evident that discontents within the game would become increasingly vocal.

As for Laker, his critical assessment of those "above" him was less confrontational than Wardle. The two men were cut from different cloth. But also, Laker, as we have seen, didn't begin working life as a miner but as a bank clerk, and this may well have influenced the way he went about making known his views. His habitual demeanour may well suggest someone who didn't go out of his way to make trouble, though, like earlier rebels, he was prepared to stick up for himself when trouble came to him.

That said, Laker can hardly be compared to any rebel of an earlier age, simply because earlier autobiographies and memoirs are alike in being either bland or unrevealing. It would be good to have known what such as "Billie" and S.F. Barnes, Bobby Peel and Tom Wass really thought about the game they played, its management, and those in authority. But they have left no written record. And those who did write their memoirs produced little more than pap, especially as professional cricketers required clearance from Lord's before they were allowed to publish their "as told to" accounts of a sportsman's life. As in other areas of English social life, no offence was to be given to the establishment. It was only with the coming of a new candour – a wider appetite for revelation nourished by the daily press and, perhaps, the arrival of commercial television – that professionals were encouraged, by publishers and agents, to divulge matters that those in charge wanted to keep under wraps. "Now it can be told." Naturally, it was easier to write with candour once you were retired. But as Laker found, that didn't prevent punitive action being taken against anyone who dared to find fault with those who for so long had considered themselves the game's true Lords and Masters.

Wardle was at least in part the architect of his own downfall. In cricket, as in other areas of life, a show of self-belief often masks a fragile ego. In Wardle's case it seems to have been inseparable from an egotistic disregard for others. Yorkshire cricketers in particular are renowned for cultivating such disregard. In their own eyes this makes them honourable rebels. In the eyes of others it makes them vainglorious bullies.

Chapter 15: The Professional Game

In January 1963 the MCC finally passed into law the abolition of the status of amateur cricketer. The change had been a long time coming and with its arrival it is natural to suppose that one of the major causes of rebellion among cricketers would be done away with. No more Gentlemen and Players. The annual fixture had anyway for some years become an empty ritual with little interest shown in it by members of the paying public, especially as the Gentlemen's team had sometimes to be bolstered by professionals. You could say that the fixture's survival represented one more instance of that English habit of bringing together the social orders in a manner intended to guarantee the continuance of the status quo. But with the passing of the new law, that particular game had to end. All cricketers were now professionals.

Cricketers have no trade union, John Arlott had written in 1948. But in 1967 the Professional Cricketers' Association came into existence. It was founded by Fred Rumsey, an amiable tun of a man, a Somerset and briefly England medium-fast bowler, and someone who proved a more than able negotiator for the Players he represented.

The newly-formed Association at once set about putting into place legally binding employment terms for all who joined it. Most importantly, Rumsey and his committee took legal advice in arranging a standard contract with agreed minimum wages for professional cricketers in England and Wales. Unsurprisingly and entirely fittingly, Arlott became the Association's first President. In commenting on this, *Wisden* noted that Arlott's "democratic views and wise counsel earned him much respect in the cricket world and among the players. His moderation and tact helped in some tight corners..." All true, and the praise is no more than that dear man deserved.

But for many the decision MCC arrived at in 1963 was not regarded as a Damascene moment. Far from it. The cricket world in England was still divided into Us and Them. S.C. Griffith (1914 – 1993) , the MCC secretary, might claim that he had nothing against Players – why, on one tour he openly confessed to having shared a room with a professional cricketer – but when in 1966 John Snow and Ken Higgs shared in a last wicket century stand of 128 against the West Indies at the Oval, it was Griffith who took care to ensure that the pair weren't photographed on the balcony holding the pints of beer with which they proposed to moisten their dry throats and, of course, celebrate their achievement. Before a shutter could click, beer glasses were exchanged for cups and saucers.

Snow provides a no-names account of this episode in *Cricket Rebel* (1976.) On the other hand, he has much to say about Griffith's influence at Sussex, where his son, Mike Griffith, was made captain in 1968. "We accepted his appointment," Snow says, "although I personally felt that carpenter's son, Tony Buss, who was some four years older, vastly more experienced and an excellent reader of the game, would have been a better choice at the time." And, going for the jugular, he adds, "[Mike Griffith] showed very little tactical flair and lacked vision. He did not understand the way people played, the fields required, or which bowlers were best for certain situations, and could not assess the way a game was shaping." (p 63.) Not an ideal captain, then.

Throughout his book, of which there will be more to say, Snow presents himself as a rebel with deep-seated and principled grievances against captains, batsmen, other bowlers, umpires … You name them, Snow has their measure, and it isn't often up. But though many of Snow's grievances were both genuine and went deep, it is difficult to share his belief that they were all principled. And in the summer of 1968 a rather more significant event than the appointment of Mike Griffith to lead Sussex indicates the limits to Snow's self-promotion of himself as a true rebel.

* * *

Here is what Snow has to say about that event, which he comes to after his passage on Mike Griffith's shortcomings and the problems which they and other issues of the season raised, some to do with the county, others with the national side and its unsatisfactory Test Series against the visiting Australians.

> Worse was to follow later in September with the
> refusal of the South African Government to accept
> Basil D'Oliveira as a member of the MCC party,
> after he had been added to the list following the
> withdrawal of Tom Cartwright with a shoulder
> injury. … It was a measure of Basil's popularity with

the team that nobody ever blamed him or
questioned his right to be in the touring party
despite, for him, a lean summer in 1968, when he
was dropped after the first Test and reappeared for
the final game only when illness caused a change in
the original selection.

There was, of course, no question of England
backing down and being dictated to by the South
African Government as to the make-up of the side.
Basil had just as much right to be in the team as any
other member despite the fact that he had
been born in Cape Town of Cape coloured parents.
If they would not accept him, there was no
alternative than to call off that particular tour, but I
question the wisdom of breaking off all official
cricketing ties with South Africa and throwing
their game into isolation. (p 64.)

It isn't easy to decide whether Snow's remarks here are
merely gauche or, as is probably the case, an attempt to
cover up his own behaviour. Either way, the words are
clumsily evasive.

In the first place, by the time he came to write his book,
Snow surely knew that Tom Cartwright's "injury" was
that honourable man's way of refusing to do the MCC's
bidding. Cartwright withdrew his name from the
announced touring party because he fully understood the
dirty politics involved in leaving D'Oliveira out of the side
and would have no truck with them. In addition, it is
scarcely credible that Snow could have been unaware that
from the moment the tour was planned, the South African
Government, who had made plain their refusal to allow

D'Oliveira to be in the party, would cancel the tour. It was, after all, common knowledge, or at all events commonly understood as a condition of the tour, that D'Oliveira should not be numbered among the tourists. Early in 1968 Sir Alec Douglas-Hume, removed as Prime-Minister in 1964 and a recent president of the MCC, learned as much from the South African PM, Vorster, whom Hume visited with the express aim of discovering whether D'Oliveira's presence in the touring party would be acceptable to the South Africans. Vorster's position was brutally simple. D'Oliveira, he said, would not be allowed in.

Given the odious Vorster's stand, which Hume duly reported to Lord's, MCC's reply should have been unequivocal. In that case, no tour. Instead, and to their eternal shame, they tried various tricks by which to leave D'Oliveira behind. He was apparently offered £20,000 if he agreed to make himself unavailable. He refused the bribe. He was dropped for the 1968 series after one Test, in which admittedly he did poorly, but what other senior player, as D'Oliveira by then was, could have expected to be so summarily dismissed? MCC clearly wanted him out of the reckoning.

But then, so desperate were England to square the series against Australia, that D'Oliveira was brought back as a last-minute substitute for the final Test. England won, largely because of D'Oliveira's massive century, an innings played in difficult conditions and with the added burden of his realisation that if he was to be in tour party he needed to succeed. The psychological strain must have been intense. He surmounted it, scored over 150, and a few days later heard over the radio, to his deep distress and to the incandescent rage of his county captain, Graveney, that he had not been chosen to tour South Africa.

Cowdrey, the captain elect, afterwards claimed he had consulted his bishop – would that he the Archbishop of Canterbury? – who thought that not choosing D'Oliveira was permissible. Cowdrey, you feel, might have done better to consult his own conscience. He might also have taken note of the fury of thousands of cricket enthusiasts at the MCC's kow-towing to the Apartheid regime. Perhaps Cowdrey did endure some spasms of a guilty conscience. He may well have squirmed at the measured disdain John Arlott expressed for the collusive tactics by means of which D'Oliveira was kept out of the proposed touring party. These tactics even included the claim that both as bowler and batsman Cartwright was more suited to South African conditions than the all-rounder brought up in them. "This may prove, perhaps to the surprise of MCC, far more than a sporting matter," Arlott wrote in the *Guardian*. It may have been one or a combination of these responses which influenced the belated, shame-faced decision to name D'Oliveira as substitute after Cartwright had withdrawn.

He was not, however, the first man they asked to step into the position vacated by Cartwright. Both Ken Higgs and Barry Knight were approached. Higgs, a decent, fast-medium bowler who began his career with Lancashire before moving to Leicester, played in fifteen Test matches between 1965-8, taking seventy-one wickets at the very good average of 20.74. His batting average of 11.56 was boosted by the sixty-three runs he scored in the famous last-wicket stand of 128 he and Snow put on against the West Indies at the Oval in 1966. Higgs was a genuine tail-ender. Barry Knight of Essex, then Leics., to whom he moved in 1967, played rather more Tests – twenty-nine in all – beginning in 1961/2 and ending in 1969, and was a lower-middle order batsman as well as a medium-fast bowler. As a Test batsman he scored a little over eight hundred runs at an average of 26.91, and his seventy wickets cost him 31.75 each. Cartwright, incidentally, played in only 5 tests – those against South Africa in the summer of 1965 – scored twenty-six runs (average 20) and took fifteen wickets at an average of 36.21. All three were good cricketers, but nobody in his right mind would think to compare any of them with D'Oliveira.

As with Cartwright before them and perhaps emboldened by his decision, Higgs and Knight both turned down the MCC's invitation to accompany the touring party. (None, it should be noted, played for England again.) Eventually, gracelessly, the MCC was left with no alternative but to invite D'Oliveira (averaging in Tests a shade over 40 with the bat and 39 with ball) to go on the tour. At which point the South African government called the tour off. The *Who's Who of Cricketers* could hardly be more disingenuous in its reporting of this moment. "When he was chosen as a member of the MCC team to tour South Africa, his acceptance caused the cancellation of the tour and brought the problem of apartheid more forcibly before the British public."

But it wasn't the British public who needed to have the "problem" brought to their attention. John Arlott, who behaved with unshakeable decency throughout this squalid episode, spoke for many if not most when he repeatedly voiced his support for D'Oliveira. In *The Little Wonder*, Robert Winder notes that the then editor of *Wisden*, Norman Preston, made clear where *his* sympathies lay: "with the congenial cricketers who had been press-ganged into isolation by political hotheads. Revisiting the relevant volumes today," Winter continues, "one is struck chiefly by the absence of a major article on the affair by John Arlott, *Wisden's* annual book reviewer." And Winder, making clear whose side he was on, reports that some years previously Arlott had actually been suspended from the BBC for his "outburst" on *Any Questions,* when as a panellist he had called the South African government, whose then prime-minister was Malan, "predominantly Nazi."

Not that this made Arlott button the lip. "Apartheid is detestable to me and I shall always oppose it," he wrote in *The Guardian,* and although Winder acknowledges that he doesn't know whether Norman Preston deliberately chose not to invite Arlott to contribute to *Wisden* in 1969 and again in 1970, or whether, as seems hardly likely, Arlott himself decided not to, he is surely right to say that "*Wisden* missed a rare chance to publish what would have been one of the great pieces of its life. It might have raised a few hackles in the more old-fashioned corners of the game (some of which could still be found at Lord's), but it would have cemented *Wisden's* moral authority around the world." (See pp 264-6 passim.)

Snow doesn't refer to Arlott in his own account of an episode that made rebels of at least John Arlott and Tom Cartwright, but he does say that "nobody" blamed D'Oliveira. What he *doesn't* say is that there were people who should have been blamed, whose hypocrisy and indifference to the moral requirement to behave well by an honourable cricketer, were, if anything, even grubbier than the tactics adopted by the cricketing establishment in the aftermath of the Bodyline controversy. Snow's evasiveness is easily explained. He had no intention of not picking up money from playing in South Africa should the chance arise, as it was soon to do. He claims to be "against apartheid and all it stands for," but then asks: "does it change the situation by turning your back on it and on the people over there who are equally opposed to separatism? I doubt it."

What this tells us is, of course, that Snow was fully prepared to go wherever money beckoned. Hence, his taking part in the private tour to South Africa organised by Derrick Robins in the autumn of 1974. Snow ties himself in knots over this. On the one hand there was the "token gesture" of allowing into the tour party the "West Indian John Shepherd of Kent and the Pakistan-born Younis Ahmed of Surrey.... They received a great welcome whenever they stepped onto a first-class field with us .... Many people told me that they never expected to see black and white mixed in a first-class match."

But the tour was unofficial. The matches surely *weren't* first class, not in England, anyway. True, the white South Africans gave them this nomenclature, but then both the apartheid government and the South African cricket authorities were desperate to achieve the respectability and recognition that went with the first-class game. From an English perspective, however, for the tour to have been first-class it would have had to be organised under the auspices of MCC, which it wasn't, though they were probably more than happy that it should go ahead. They may well have seen the tour as a way of softening up the public in the UK for the prospect of a future tour by the white South Africans. "Look, when we tour there we can take players of colour and it's alright."

If so, they were at best deluding themselves, at worst hoping to delude others despite what they knew. It's difficult to credit that any of them could have believed

Vorster and his fellow-politicians would change their minds about allowing non-whites into the South African team. The implication, that somehow Robins' tours – there was more than one during the decade – therefore constituted a successful rebellion against apartheid won't wash. Crowds in South Africa might applaud players from Pakistan and the West Indies who were part of a visiting side, but there was never any chance that under apartheid Black or Cape-Coloured Africans would be allowed to play for South Africa.

It is, however, to be noted that Robins' tours were arranged *after* the South Africans were refused the chance to tour England in 1970. The prospect of this tour prompted much misgiving among sports writers and the general public. Though some insisted, as they always do, that sport and politics shouldn't be mixed, it was apparent to most that at the very least the coming tour would not merely be contentious, it would certainly cause protests. For some time Lord's chose not to listen. Despite urgings from the government and from various dignitaries, including the Archbishop of Canterbury and the Chief Rabbi, the Cricket Council voted for the tour to go ahead. Finally, at what was almost the midnight hour, the Home Secretary, James Callaghan, insisted that the tour be cancelled. He was worried by the possibility, even probability, of rebellious protests against the tourists and of violence at the grounds where they would be appearing. Moreover, there was a general election in the offing. It would not look good to its supporters for a Labour government to appear to be in support, if only passively, of Apartheid.

English cricket as a whole does not come well out of this episode. Had there been a rebellion from within the game itself, it would have been a populist one of the right, given that the majority of players wanted the tour to proceed, though the president of the Cricketers' Association was opposed to it. Indeed, Arlott went so far as to announce that, should the tour go ahead, he would refuse to act as a BBC Test Match commentator. Here, as so often, he emerges as a rebel against the cricketing establishment, though one without histrionics, content to put the unanswerable case against apartheid. It was, after all, Arlott who had managed to get Basil D'Oliveira out of South Africa and make it possible for his cricketing talents to flourish in England. And it was Arlott who, when asked by Customs at a South African airport which race he belonged to, answered "Human."

* * *

With the South African tour cancelled, a series was arranged between England and the Rest of the World, led by Gary Sobers. After the series was concluded at the Oval, England's captain, Ray Illingworth, made a silly speech in which he said he hoped that South Africa would soon be allowed back into the cricketing community. His words were loudly booed by the many West Indian supporters who had congregated for the closing ceremonies. Illingworth's startled look, modulating into a fleeting, embarrassed smile, suggested that he hadn't anticipated this hostile response to what he must have thought were unexceptionable words. But then in cricket, as in other walks of life, rebels in one context can be reactionaries in another. By the time he became captain of England, and a very good one at that, Illingworth had moved from Yorkshire to Leicester, where, as captain for a number of seasons, he was remarkably successful in turning a mediocre club into one of high achievements. Here, then, we need to consider why Illingworth made the move, one that has about it more than a whiff of rebelliousness.

According to the *Who's Who of Cricketers*, "a difference between Illingworth and the Yorkshire Club at the end of 1968 let to his appointment as captain of Leicestershire in 1969." Illingworth, a proud man who from his early days had been an outstanding all-rounder for Yorkshire – he achieved the double on no fewer than six occasions between 1957-1964 – was also a prickly one; he seems to have had several fallings-out with the County Committee, and he felt justifiable anger at the Committee's high-handed treatment of its players. On one occasion his wife had been ordered off the Players' balcony by that autocratic, puffed-up parody of a Gentleman, Brian Sellers.

But the immediate cause of Illingworth's decision to leave the club to which he had given long years of distinguished service was Yorkshire's refusal to offer him a three-year contract, to which he quite reasonably felt he was entitled. Leicestershire took advantage of the Yorkshire Committee's mulish behaviour by coming in with the three-year contract Illingworth considered his due, and for a sizeable time afterwards he was still signing three-year contracts with them. His rebellion against the Yorkshire Committee's obduracy did him no harm and it did Leicestershire a great deal of good.

At a guess, Brian Close, born a year earlier than Illingworth, and a friend, similarly rebelled against what he took to be the misguided ways of authority. Close, as is well known, was an adept at not toeing the line. In fact, he frequently went looking for lines he could refuse to toe. "In 1966 he was given the English captaincy and looked to be set for a long reign when suddenly he was at loggerheads with the authorities and his international career abruptly ended." This report by the *Who's Who of Cricketers* is restrained about the reasons for Close's losing the England captaincy. It was, in fact, brought about by Lord's strong disapproval of his extravagant time-wasting tactics in a County game against Warwickshire. Nor is it entirely correct. Close did return to the England side, though never again as captain. It seems odd that whoever was responsible for producing the entry on Close in the *Who's Who* didn't recall one of the more infamous remarks made by an English cricketer, Tony Greig's prophecy at the start of the 1976 series against the West Indies, that "I intend, with the help of Closey and some others, to make them grovel." Some hopes. All the grovellings were, in fact, England's, though as an England batsman Close had the dubious pleasure of exposing his body to a constant barrage from the outstanding West Indian fast bowlers on that tour.

Close came near to wrecking his own career on more than one occasion. However, his rebellious move to Somerset in 1970 brought him and the County he captained for several years a measure of continued success he had not enjoyed with Yorkshire. He did as well by Somerset, another run-of-the-mill county, as Illingworth did by Leicestershire.

But rebels against those in command of their native county though they were, both Illingworth and Close were in most respects natural conservatives. Illingworth really couldn't see why South Africa should have been banned from playing international cricket; Close is on record as saying that young Asian cricketers in Yorkshire were unlikely to make the grade because they had no "work" in them. This prejudice, one it is difficult to avoid calling at least unconsciously racist, was deeply engrained in certain Yorkshire cricketers and their ilk. The appalling Yorkshireman, Don Mosey, one time BBC Test Match Commentator, spoke of Asian diet as featuring "rat curry." (For which, to the BBC's credit, he was promptly removed from the airwaves.) Even worse was the moment when Viv Richards, playing against Yorkshire for his adopted county of Somerset, was sauntering back to the pavilion at Headingley at the end of his innings when he was ordered by someone in the crowd to "get a move on, you black bastard." Richards sprinted in the direction of the caller, though the moron had enough sense to decamp before Richards could get to him. The episode prompted Ian Botham, rightly loyal to Richards, his team mate, and rebelling against conservative proprieties, to announce that he was more than prepared never to play at Headingley again.

A rebel of the heart, the hard-living, hard-playing Botham in many ways recalls the kind of cricketer Cardus extolled, though it's doubtful he would have found words of praise for this new breed of hero. Botham belongs to a period in cricket very unlike Cardus's golden age. He was not merely a highly visible presence, a cricketer known to people who had no interest in the game that made him famous. His fame brought him wealth that would have been inconceivable to, say, MacLaren or Parkin or Tyldesley. And whereas in former times nobody would think to put wealth and cricket in the same sentence, by the later years of the twentieth century it was by no means uncommon for cricketers to be able to make a good living not merely from the game they played but from trading on the reputation their prowess brought them. After his heroics at Headingley in 1981 Botham was signed up for TV Weetabix advertisements, a cereal it's difficult to imagine often featured as part of his breakfast.

By then, though, cricketers were becoming used to the money which advertising and sponsorship brought them. They were profiting, in all senses of the word, from numerous acts of rebellion that affected English cricket from the 1970s on, when player power was used to overcome the sclerotic bodies of County Committees.

Here, a further point needs to be made by way of qualifying the earlier remarks about Illingworth. When he was asked to act as captain of the MCC touring team to Australia in 1970/1, he was summoned to Lord's to discuss the composition of the side. Once there, he discovered that at least some members were deeply opposed to including D'Oliveira. Presumably, he was held responsible for the cancellation of the South African tour two years previously. Illingworth insisted that he wanted D'Oliveira in his party, and, after some wrangling, he got his way. Geoffrey Boycott, who reported on the radio having this story from Illingworth himself, added that "If the captain wants you, he gets you." And without naming names he made clear that had Cowdrey stood up for D'Oliveira in 1968, then D'Oliveira would have been named in the original party to tour South Africa.

Thinking about this, it occurs to me that Illingworth emerges from this story with the kind of credit Benny Goodman should be given for employing black musicians in his great orchestra of the late 1930s. Goodman was famously called "colour-blind," not so much because he took what would then have been a radical stance on racial equality as because he wanted the best musicians to play for him. Lionel Hampton, Teddy Wilson, Billie Holiday, were the best. Therefore they joined the Goodman Orchestra. D'Oliveira was a class cricketer, therefore Illingworth insisted he go on tour to Australia. It was the ones who wanted "to keep politics out of sport" who were guilty of bringing politics into it.

* * *

Near the end of *Cricket Rebel*, Snow has a chapter called "What is wrong with cricket organisation." The title suggests that we are in for a further exercise in the special pleading that mars much of his book. But as it turns out, the chapter is richly informative in revealing how, especially during the season of 1975, county cricketers were on the brink of organising strikes that would have brought the game to a halt. The Committees at Lancashire and Worcestershire, in particular, found themselves confronted with rebellion to an extent reminiscent of what had happened in Notts in 1881, though it may be more relevant to note that a year earlier, in 1974, Major League Baseball in the USA had been threatened by a unanimous players' strike, which had led to greatly improved salaries and terms of employment for all.

The resentment among England's cricketers about terms and conditions, while perhaps not unanimous, was certainly widespread. According to Snow, "Worcestershire players went so far as to inform their committee of their intention to down bats unless they were given an early promise that their frustrations and long drawn out differences would be aired. I understand that only a last minute dash by Jimmy James, the Lancashire secretary, averted a similar situation when Lancashire were on the point of striking." (p 179.)

Bafflingly – unless he or his publishers were worried about the possibilities of a libel action – Snow adds primly that "I will not comment on the issues involved." Would that he had. But despite this uncharacteristic reticence, he scatters enough clues for us to understand that the issues certainly involved contracts, salaries, and terms of employment, all matters in which the Players felt they had a right to expect some form of negotiation. Such rights were not so much disputed as waved away by County Committees. The Committees took for granted that they deserved unquestioning loyalty and subservience from those they hired and, when it suited them, fired. As to this latter right, Snow reports what he fairly calls the "disgraceful episode" in which Sussex's loyal player, Ken Suttle, was told in 1970 that his contract would not be renewed. "Ken heard about it in the most casual way, when Eddie Harrison, then chairman of the cricket committee, caught him walking up the roadway at the back of the pavilion [at Hove.] Ken later told me the news came in the following manner: 'Hello, Ken, I've been meaning to have a word with you. How's the wife and family? All right, I hope. Oh, by the way, you're not being re-engaged for next season.'" (*Cricket Rebel,* pp 183-4.)

Behaviour such as Harrison's is liable to make a rebel out of the most loyal of men. And it is with such casual, boorish indifference to the dignity of professional cricketers in mind, that we can perhaps best understand the appeal of Kerry Packer to those who played cricket for a living.

Chapter 16: New Directions

Given the steadily growing and sometimes near-explosive unrest over players' contracts during the 1970s on which John Snow touches, the Kerry Packer Affair, as it is sometimes known, was perfectly of its moment. In view of its lasting impact, it should come as no surprise that several books have been devoted to the subject. In addition, there has been much comment from cricketing journalists; and cricketers, too, especially those most closely involved with it, have had their say. What follows is therefore a bare-bones summary, one which focusses on the rebelliousness the Affair drew on and inevitably fomented.

Kerry Packer was the son of an Australian media tycoon. At the time of the Centenary Test between Australia and England at Melbourne, he was trying to persuade the Australian Cricket Board of Control to give him exclusive rights to televise the match and others on Channel 9, which he owned. Unwisely, in view of what then happened, The Board of Control said no. Packer, refusing to take that for an answer, entered into secret negotiations with England's captain, Tony Greig, to get him and other international cricketers to sign a deal which would guarantee them good money if they agreed to play a quasi-Test series of matches that Channel 9 would televise in full. Four England players were signed up: Greig, Knott, Underwood, and Snow.

Then thirteen Australians announced that they, too, had signed. Soon after that further English cricketers, including Bob Woolmer and Dennis Amiss, were recruited, and before you could say Grace, Richie Benaud let it be known that he was the originator of the idea, that what he had done was in the interest of ensuring good money for all players involved, and that the pop-up organisation known as "World Series Cricket" would stage international matches whose attractions would far outweigh those of conventional Test matches, especially as the best players from most if not all nations had signed to play.

Well, not all of them had done so. Quite a few of the England team on tour didn't sign. Derek Randall, who scored that magical 174 in the Centenary Test, was among those who for one reason or another did not put pen to paper. (Greig afterwards said he didn't invite Randall to join the other rebels because the young man was at the outset of his international career and Greig didn't want to do harm to his future prospects.)

Packer also failed to land a much bigger name. Vanity required Geoffrey Boycott to make clear that he had indeed been approached but, he said, he had unhesitatingly chosen to declare himself loyal to his country in its hour of need. Mighty big of him, especially as he had *not* made himself available two seasons earlier, when Lillee and Thomson had been at their fastest. On that occasion Boycott had announced that he owed it to himself to escape what he was pleased to call the "pressures and tensions" of international cricket and instead devote himself to the awesome responsibilities of the Yorkshire captaincy. Fewer pressures and tensions there, apparently, and no mention of the fact that, Australian fast bowlers apart, there was the little matter of Boycott having been passed over for the English captaincy, which had instead gone to Kent's Mike Denness (1940 – 2013), a batsman of far lesser ability and someone for whom Boycott scarcely bothered to hide his contempt.

Boycott was still Yorkshire's captain in 1977, but with so many of the world's best fast bowlers signed up for Packer the pressures and tensions of playing for England had considerably eased, and under the captaincy of Brearley, who had replaced the sacked Greig, who had himself replaced Denness as England's captain, Boycott graciously announced his readiness to resume his career as "England's premier batsman."

This was the title Boycott gave himself. So, at all events, I was told years ago by an artist friend who had been present when a Visiting MCC team played a fixture against a well-known school in the area of York. Boycott, who had agreed to appear as a guest for the School team – the headmaster was an ex-County cricketer – arrived early and, having fished a herbal tea-bag from his capacious bag and arranged for it to be prepared for later consumption, changed, went out onto the pavilion steps and enquired of the gaggle of boys waiting there, "Who's going to bowl to England's premier batsman, then?" And off to the nets he marched.

Almost an hour passed before he left. The match was now about to commence. As had been previously agreed, the school would bat first, and as was further agreed, Boycott would open with the Headmaster. Oh, and it had also been agreed that if either batsman reached his half-century he would retire. The headmaster, having reached his fifty, made way for number three. Boycott reached his fifty and went on batting. It was only after the headmaster's strenuous reminders of their prior agreement that England's premier batsman finally, and with apparent reluctance, left the field.

At tea he was asked what he would like to drink. England's premier batsman explained that he could drink no other infusion than the one he required to be made from the tea bag he produced from his pocket. He then spent some time wondering aloud how England's premier batsman could be treated with less than total respect by the media, the MCC, and anyone else who came to mind.

Although there may be apocryphal elements in this story, and it almost certainly gained in the re-telling, it does point to a quality which most who have observed Boycott's career agree is at the core of his achievements both on and off the field. This is, that Boycott never did anything that wasn't intended to further the career of Geoffrey Boycott. Few who saw his running out of Randall at Trent Bridge in the summer of 1977, when Randall was playing in his first Test there, are likely to forget or forgive an act of such selfishness. Boycott's making himself available again for England in the summer of 1977 certainly helped him in his determination to score his hundredth century, which he duly did against a weakened Australian attack at Headingley. Three years later, this man of professed loyalty to the English cause signed up for the rebel tour to South Africa, as a result of which he was banned from playing for England for three years. Most unfair, he considered that to be, pointing out that had he played in more Tests he could have scored even more runs and probably improved his average into the bargain. But as the Australian joke goes: "How many runs did Boycott score for England? Answer: two. All the rest were for Boycott."

* * *

Most commentators on the Packer Affair tend to regard the man himself as more villain than hero. Certainly, he was in it for the money. But as we have seen, cricketing authorities, including County Committees, tended to treat the Players under contract to them with a disregard for their feelings which was bound to breed deep resentment. (Among the honourable exceptions were Essex and Hampshire.) Here then it's appropriate to recall the bitterness Joe Hardstaff felt at the way he was treated at the end of his long and distinguished career at Notts. Not a single committee member, he said, could be bothered to thank him. He simply got on his bike and rode away.

Hardstaff retired in 1955. Fifteen years later, as John Snow reports, Ken Suttle came in for even more brutish treatment at the hands of the Sussex Committee. And it is worth noting that at Taunton in the same year, 1970, Tom Cartwright, newly arrived from Warwickshire, was ordered by a Somerset Committee member to remove the sticker in the back window of the car Cartwright had parked outside the pavilion at the county ground. "We don't allow politics here," the man told him. *Vote Labour*, the sticker said. It's a fair bet that had the sticker promoted the Conservative cause nothing would have been said. As it was, Cartwright's time at Somerset ended when he had a heated argument with the chairman of the County Committee, who accused him of being unfit. Cartwright went on to Glamorgan as a coach and in 1976 played a handful of games for that county. Then he retired.

* * *

The overwhelming majority of those who made up the organizing committees in cricket, from the smallest county to Lord's, were and maybe still are, dyed-in-the-wool conservatives. Some have a genuine passion for cricket. Other simply see themselves as "the right sort" to run cricket. No wonder cricketers have rebelled against the kind of treatment all too often meted out to them. The wonder is rather that there haven't been more rebellions. As to why there haven't been, until the 1970s John Arlott's explanation – that cricketers are basically Romantic in disposition – will go some distance to accounting for their customary, near fatalistic acceptance of how they were treated.

But there is also the obvious fact that Players were by and large recruited from working-class circumstances and, as W.H. Auden remarked in his Elegy on the poet W.B. Yeats, "the poor have the sufferings to which they are fairly accustomed." That, however, was in 1939, and six years later the poor were finding accustomed sufferings anything but fair. The gradual freeing of cricket from the assumptions of an eternal, unchanging "Englishness" – of rurality, squires and peasants (or Gentlemen and Players), of subservience – meant that only by the 1970s were new freedoms and rights coming into operation; and even then the transition from one age to another was by no means smooth. How could it be? There were many vested interests involved, many inherited prejudices to be overcome. Packer's brash intervention was less, surely, the catalyst for change than a spectacular instance of it.

But look at photographs of cricketers themselves from the 1980s to the present day, and then compare them to photographs of cricketers from the previous thirty or forty years. See how short back and sides have been exchanged for a plethora of hair styles, including those which for a season were modish, for after-seasons most dated: Bob Willis's attempt to ape Bob Dylan's bushiness, Botham's "mullet," other, even more outlandish, cuts; look at the logos beginning to appear on shirts and trousers; notice such brand signs as Phil Edmond's Swatch watch. Look at the sponsored cars drawn up behind the pavilions of county grounds. We are a long way from Compton's handsome face, hair immaculately groomed, peering down from hoardings, for which in 1947 Brylcreem paid him a rumoured £1500. Since the Packer Affair cricket has become a marketable business from which all professionals can make money.

* * *

In 1970 most cricketers would, if given the chance, have voted for the tour of England by the all-white South African team to go ahead. This doesn't mean they can be accused of racist bigotry. By then, more than one county had on its playing staff cricketers who came from Afro-Caribbean or Asian countries. In that year, for example, Gordon Greenidge joined Hampshire, where he would soon supplant Roy Marshall, who had been with the county from 1953 and who would finish two years later, in which year Bishan Bedi joined Northants., a county which already had as opening bowler Malik Sarfraz Nawaz. Also in 1972 Syed Zaheer Abbas became a Gloucestershire player, and Alvin Kallicheran signed for Warwickshire, playing in the same side as Rohan Kanhai, who had been with the county since 1968. 1968 was the year in which

Carlton Forbes was joined at Notts by the incomparable Garfield Sobers, and again in 1968 Clive Lloyd began a long and successful career with Lancs. as did the Indian wicket-keeper, Farouk Engineer.

As far as is known, these, and other, more run-of-the-mill players, seem to have integrated without difficulty into the county sides for whom they player. Familiarity by and large bred content. At the time some commentators rebuked cricketers of all stripes for not having done more to oppose the 1970 tour. But while they can perhaps be faulted for political quietism, the vast majority stood neither to gain nor to lose from the tour. If they thought it should have gone ahead it wasn't because they expected the tour to fill their pockets with randgold.

But a few years later, the Packer Affair divided dressing rooms up and down the country. There were rebels now on both sides. And money assuredly was an issue. As Robert Winder notes, in 1977 "Everyone knew cricketers were not well paid, so it wasn't hard [for Packer and his agents] to sign up 35 leading stars." (*The Little Wonder,* p 277.)

Money wasn't however the only issue, or rather, it wasn't merely a question of how much Packer could pay the players he had signed. When Sussex made public their intention to re-appoint Tony Greig to the county captaincy in 1978, even though he had been dismissed as England captain, Nottinghamshire and Lancashire proposed to MCC that Sussex should be removed from the county championship. Kent chose to take the captaincy away from Asif Iqbal, one of the Packer players, but as Birley says "they were careful not to try to dispense with his services as a player." (*Social History of Cricket* p 318.)

This was not merely because Aqbal was an outstanding cricketer. It was also because legal advice to all counties was that the cricketers involved in playing in the Packer World Series had not by doing so broken their county contracts. To dismiss them would certainly bring court action and any county which tore up a valid contract would find itself faced with bills it couldn't afford to pay. Packer had top-class lawyers at his disposal. As a show of strength he employed them on behalf of Greig and Mike Proctor (of South Africa and Gloucestershire), threatening to take the Test and County Cricket Board to court, claiming restraint of trade. Tangling with Packer was, it soon became apparent, a costly business.

How then to counter the threat he was seen as posing? Wait until contracts ran out, the lawyers said, that was when the day of atonement would come. At that moment the rebels who had signed up for Packer could be legally shown the door. A good thing, too, according to the diehards, among whom was the then editor of *Wisden*, Norman Preston. He used the 1978 Annual to let his readers know that he could no longer tell if cricketers were players or mercenaries. I suspect that at the base of this accusation was Preston's belief that those who had signed for Packer had abandoned all principles for mere self-interest. They had become hirelings, rebels against decency. But they weren't. They were rebels against a structure which kept them, so they must have felt, in a condition of near servility, and then cast them off when their usefulness was past. Off you go, Hardstaff. Out you go, Suttle.

But anyway, the legal advice to wait for a day of atonement made little sense for counties in desperate need of the talents of cricketers who had signed to Packer's World Series. Unsurprisingly, therefore, several counties announced that when contracts came up for renewal their own Packer rebels would be given the chance to sign new ones. A sensible precautionary tactic, this, given that County Committees were made aware that if they chose to let their rebels go, other counties, less committed to outlawing the rebels, would in all likelihood snap them up.

There was, however, something of a crisis at Warwickshire when the Committee announced that it would not renew Dennis Amiss's contract. Amiss, a leading batsman and a Test cricketer who played fifty Tests for England in which he averaged 46.30, had joined the Packer circus and as a consequence was put into virtual purdah by his county colleagues. They would have nothing to do with him, banished him to a corner of the changing-room, or so it was rumoured, and wouldn't speak to him on or off the field; they wanted him out. They sent a jointly-signed letter to the Committee saying as much, and the Committee responded by remarking that, if this was what they wanted, then Amiss would not be offered a new contract when his expired, as it was shortly to do.

This is a strange use of player power. The organised action of Worcester players about which John Snow writes, and which was referred to in the previous chapter, makes good sense. They wanted better pay and conditions. It's more difficult to understand why Amiss's team mates should have ganged up on him, and given that one of them, Geoff Humpage, would only a few years later sign for a rather less excusable enterprise, it seems utterly baffling. A case of mistaken resentment? Loyalty to a cause? But if so, what cause, exactly? Doing the bidding of those who owe you little by way of loyalty seems decidedly odd. I have tried talking to more than one Warwickshire stalwart who played for the county at that time, and the most I have learnt is that "there was more to it than met the eye."

But if the players were against Amiss, the Members felt very differently. Kallicheran always excepted, Amiss was Warwickshire's best batsman. (He finished with an overall average of 43.28.) Why on earth should the County want to get rid of him, the members wanted to know? A special meeting to discuss the issue was called, and then, at Amiss's own request, called off. Tempers cooled and in due course Amiss the Rebel – a most unusual collocation for so affably mild a man – was reinstated. Ruffled feathers were smoothed. The atmosphere in changing rooms improved. The worst effects of the Packer Affair seemed to be over.

But something worse than World Series Cricket was about to happen. The 1980s saw a series of "Rebel" tours of South Africa and with these came fresh problems.

* * *

The Packer circus, which brought with it such gimmicks as night cricket and coloured clothing, nevertheless benefited professional cricketers in England. Not that this was Packer's intention, but the high salaries he was able to offer to the cricketers he recruited almost certainly helped other, less-favoured players, because County Committees found themselves needing to discover the financial means to keep their cricketers from walking away, and this required them to show comparable if not identical consideration to all their contracted players. Packer wouldn't have had this in mind when he dreamt up his World Series Cricket. In the deliberately quaint words of a correspondent in *The Guardian,* he was "a bounder and a cad," one who didn't play by MCC rules. But the consequences of his intervention did on the whole benefit cricketers.

The same can hardly be said of the "Rebel" tours of South Africa. Most of the cricketers who took part in these tours undoubtedly benefited financially, though in the long run the careers and even lives of some were ruined. We are here only concerned with the English tours, but we should note that the West Indian tour parties to South Africa of 1982-3 and again 1983-4 resulted in the ostracising of most of the players in their own islands, and at least one of them finished as a down-and-out druggie. Nor did the tours, including those by Australian and Singhalese teams, make an iota of difference to the brutal treatment of South African blacks by the apartheid government under P.W. Botha.

What did, was the decision in 1989 by the new South African prime minister, De Klerk, to release Nelson Mandela from his twenty-seven years of captivity. De Klerk's action not only made a welcome mockery of Margaret Thatcher's prediction that "Those who expect change to come to South Africa in our life-time are living in cloud-cuckoo land," it resulted in financial and other disasters for the tour side led by Gatting which at the time of the announcement had newly arrived from England. Well, good.

But in 1981, nearly a decade before the fiasco of what proved to be the final rebel tour, a cricketing party intent on going to South Africa was put together in great secrecy. Led by Graham Gooch, the party, known by those hostile to it as "The Dirty Dozen," in fact numbered fifteen players. Apart from Gooch himself they included Amiss, who, having had his England career terminated by signing for Packer may well have felt that by then he had nothing left to lose, Boycott (he of the "principled" stand against Packer), Emburey, Hendrick, Humpage, Knott, Larkins, John Lever, Old, Sidebottom, Les Taylor, Underwood, Willey, and Woolmer. As soon as their identities were known to the

MCC, all received three-year bans from international cricket, which at least had the virtue of ending Boycott's career as a Test cricketer, though no doubt the blow was softened by the amount of randgold he and the others received from various backers, including South African Breweries, under which soubriquet the rebel party played.

No World Series Cricket, this. Those who went to South Africa did not go in defiant and excusable pursuit of trade. Instead, they skulked off in search of what, to put the matter bluntly, amounted to blood money. Hence, Kit Wright's excoriating poem, "I Found South African Breweries Most Hospitable," which begins:

> Meat smell of blood in locked rooms I cannot smell it,
> Screams of the brave in torture loges I never heard
> > nor heard of
> Apartheid I wouldn't know how it spell it,
> None of these things am I paid to believe a word of
> For I am a stranger to cant and contumely.
> I am a professional cricketer.
> My only consideration is my family.

And it ends:

> They keep falling out of windows they must be clumsy
> And unprofessional not that anyone told me,
> Spare me your wittering spare me your whimsy,
> Sixty thousand pounds is what they sold me
> And I have no brain. I am an anomaly.
> I am a professional cricketer.
> My only consideration is my family.

The moral squalor of these tours is beyond dispute. It's one thing not to feel the need to protest when a White South African team comes on tour to a nation which, officially at least, treats citizens of whatever colour and ethnic origins as equal. It's quite another to take money from a set-up where the majority of the inhabitants are a brutalised under-class. The rebels who went on tour in 1981-2 could only not have known the reality of life for millions of Black South Africans if, as Kit Wright suggests, they had no brain. Assuming they all did, even if some of their brains were pitifully small, their willing co-operation in such a tour is shameful. Rebels? Yes, against decency. The English cricketers who chose to sign up for the tour Graham Gooch led are to principled rebellion what sump-oil is to wine.

At one point early on in the Gatting-led tour of South Africa, a television camera happened to be present when a young Black man with blood on his shirt from a beating by a white policeman approached Gatting himself to show him his injuries. Did Gatting realise what was being done to protesters, the man asked? Gatting turned away, muttering words among which, some who overheard them later reported, was at least one expletive. The following day he insisted that as the violence took place outside the ground it had nothing to do with him. He was in South Africa to play cricket.

The rest of his squad comprised Athey, Barnett, Chris Broad, Chris Cowdrey (whose father had defended the omission of D'Oliveira from the cancelled 1968-9 tour), Dilley, Ellison, Emburey, Foster, French, Jarvis, Maynard, Tim Robinson, Greg Thomas, Alan Wells and, as player/manager, David Graveney. Because of the protests, few spectators turned up for such games as were played, and the tour left the hosts badly out of pocket.

Again, a three-year ban on playing international cricket was instituted against squad members, after which the egregious Gatting was re-instated in the Test team, and Emburey, Jarvis, Foster and Wells were all allowed to play for England. Unlike the Bourbons, of whom it was said they forgot nothing from their various, often disastrous, experiences, and learnt nothing, the MCC, while assuredly learning nothing, chose to forget everything. It did them no harm. At least some of the rebels from the two tours have prospered from the game they disgraced. Gooch and Gatting have been welcomed back into the establishment, and the incorrigible Boycott, who is presumably responsible for the fact that he is invariably introduced on air as "Former England Captain" – he captained four times – is allowed to blather on in the Test Commentary Box, his contributions largely taken up with an unstoppable recitation of his own virtues intertwined with claims for an unrivalled, far-sighted sagacity.

It is, therefore, worth recalling the words of Matthew Engel, who was editor of *Wisden* in 1992, when South Africa was re-admitted to international cricket. "Nothing in cricket had disgraced the game over the years so much as its relationship with South Africa," he wrote. And he was especially angered by the dropping of David Gower from England's Test team while John Emburey, who had been on both the 1981-2 and 1989 tours, was recalled. "Short of standing on the square at Lord's and giving a V-sign to the Long Room, it is hard to show how anyone can have shown greater unconcern," he said. It should be said, though, that Emburey had no call to offer the V-sign to Lord's, given that forgiveness for him was, as Engel also says, "immediate." He had more reason to thank them.

As for the dropping of Gower, one of the most elegant of post-war English batsmen, as well as one of the most successful, and certainly one who brought pleasure to all who saw him bat, you almost feel he was being punished for what the guilty must have regarded as his disdainful turning away from their acts of malfeasance.

Last Over

Cricketing rebels once risked a good deal for the causes they variously championed or, on other occasions, protested against. It is difficult to think nowadays of circumstances similar to those that drove such cricketers as Bobby Peel and Billy Barnes from the game. However headstrong and misguided they and such later rebels as Harold Larwood and Johnny Wardle may sometimes have been, they went their own way in defiance of what some might have called prudent counsel, and their rebelliousness, which was often principled, came at a price.

And nowadays? Perhaps the most spectacular case of a contemporary rebel is Kevin Pietersen, who, when he was briefly captain of England, managed to get the then national coach given his marching orders, though he himself subsequently lost the captaincy and then, more recently, found himself extra to requirement as far as Test cricket goes. But whatever the rights and wrongs of his dismissal from England's Test team, Pietersen has not suffered financially. On the contrary, he has been rewarded with a fat contract to play Indian Premier League cricket.

Pietersen is therefore in a line of rebels which begins with Kerry Packer's covert plans. Money rather than cricketing considerations propels the kind of rebellion which Pietersen's choices typify. And although mouth-service is repeatedly paid to the "honour" of playing for your national side, the reality is very different. Money may have been a motivating factor among some of the earlier cricketing rebels, but as we have seen their major concerns were for the most part other than financial, though money-matters weren't always excluded from behaviour which was variously stroppy, unbiddable, idealistic, recalcitrant, eccentric, long-sighted, disinterested, or plain mulish.

"Now God stand up for bastards." Edmund's words in *King Lear* are spoken on behalf of men born out of wedlock, but they will do to cover at least some of the rebels mentioned in *The Awkward Squad*. And if God won't stand up for them, someone else should. For these and the other rebels with whom this book has been concerned were to have an often profound influence on the game of cricket, even if their masters plainly wished otherwise. They helped to shape its fortunes, were responsible for many of the changes made in the course of its history, ranging from cricket's Laws, through conditions of employment, to nomenclature. For these and other reasons, they deserve to be remembered.

* * *

It's difficult not to feel that rather more wisdom from County Committees might have averted some of the brouhahas that began to envelop cricket from the 1970s on. But for this to have happened would have required such Committees to be made up of the kind of men who were for the most part conspicuous by their absence. Besides, rebellion in the sense of refusing to accept unquestioningly any and all of Authority's diktats now seems intrinsic to the game. Not even the introduction of neutral umpires into Test cricket has prevented the kind of challenge to that once sacrosanct and unshakeable agreement between cricketers that the umpire's decision is final. Hence, closed-circuit TV reviews of umpires' decisions. And as we saw at the beginning of the book, if, as never used to be the case, umpires have their decisions challenged – or so we are asked to believe by those who tend to ignore any suggestion of W.G. Grace's sharp practice (and that of others who could be cited) – it is no wonder that umpires themselves should begin to rebel. Disputes between umpires and players are now commonplace. There is an old story about the bowler who had every appeal for an LBW turned down by the umpire standing at his end. Front foot, back foot, plumb in front, it made no difference. "Not out", was the reply to the bowler's every shout. Finally, he got one through the batsman's guard and out went the middle stump. The bowler turned with a look of mild frustration to the umpire. "Nearly got him that time," he said.

No, it wasn't Larwood. Nor, of course, could it be a bowler of the twenty-first century, because such a bowler would on most international occasions have his appeal referred to the replay cameras. Only India opposes the replay system, and even India allows its partial use. But if these and other technical aids, which may or may not include light meters, quell the potential for some occasions of rebellious behaviour, they cannot guarantee that all rebellions will disappear from the game. The spirit of cricket includes elements which, sometimes impish, sometimes devilish, choose or need to challenge the limits of what at any one time is reckoned acceptable. On the one hand the Law-givers. On the other, the rebels.

CODA

At the time of the 1984-5 Miners' Strike, the Derbyshire folksinger/songwriter, John Young, who with his son and daughter Paddy and Christy Young form the folk-song trio *The Grey Picker,* composed "Larwood", which was sung on a number of marches. The words, best performed to its lovely, lilting tune that can be heard on the CD *Namaste,* are as follows:

> Heroes in white and cricket ball flying,
> New world trying to forget the years
> Of waste and shame, look to a game,
> And a long summer sunshine to dry an empire's tears.
>
> Out of the darkness steps a young miner,
> None finer at bowling the ball;
> Shyness and dreams, to leave the coal seams
> And breathe in the clean air, not the dust of coal.
>
> Faster than any, any before you,
> They called it war and cursed your name.
> "Larwood the killer"! Larwood the hangman"!
> Because you squared up Bradman and showed his
> mortal frame.

The English gentry! How manly! How gentle!
How must you resent! How England forgot!
The war was over and they blamed the soldier,
Demanded he said sorry for firing the shot.

Far from Trent Bridge now, a home at last found
By the ground where they cursed your name.
On Sydney Hill, echoing still
In the dreams of a hero who deserved more than shame.

The Grey Picker, *Namaste,* John Young Consulting Lts 2010.
I offer my grateful thanks to Rodney Bickerstaffe for pointing
me in the direction of the CD and to John Young for providing
me with a copy of the recording.

Selected Bibliography

Arlott, John, *Concerning Cricket,* (1949)
  Cricket in the Counties, (1950)

Birley, Derek, *The Willow Wand: Some Cricket Myths
  Explored* (1979)
  A Social History of Cricket (1999)

Bailey, P, Thorn, P. and Wynne-Thomas, P, *Who's Who
  of Cricketers* (1984)

Bright-Holmes, John, *Lords & Commons: Cricket in
  Novels and Stories* (1988)

Cardus, Neville, *Autobiography* (1947)
  Cricket All the Year (1952)

Carr, J.L. *Dictionary of Extraordinary Cricketers* (n.d.
  poss. 1986)

Daft, Richard, *Kings of Cricket* (n d. 1880?)

De Selincourt, Hugh, *The Game of the Season* (1931)

Dexter, Ted and Makins, Clifford, *Testkill* (1976)

Foot, David, *Cricket's Unholy Trinity* (1985)

Grace, W.G., *Cricketing Reminiscences and Personal
  Recollections* (1899)

Hamilton, Duncan, *Harold Larwood* (2009)

Hammond, Walter, *Cricket's Secret History* (1952)

Hawke, Lord, *Recollections and Reminiscences,* (1924)

Haynes, NB, and Lucas, John, *The Trent Bridge Battery* (1985)

Heald, Tim, *Village Cricket* (2004)

Hobsbawm, Eric, *Uncommon People: Resistance, Rebellion, and Jazz* (1961)

Horspool, David, *The English Rebel* (2009)

Imlach, Garry, *My Father and Other Working-Class Football Heroes* (2005)

Knox, Malcolm, *Never a Gentlemen's Game* (2012)

Le Quesne, Laurence, *The Bodyline Controversy* (1983)

Lilley, Arthur, *Twenty Four Years of Cricket* (1912)

Lucas, E.V., *100 Years of Trent Bridge* (1938)

Marshall, John, *The Duke Who Was Cricket* (1961)

H.H. Montgomery, *Old Cricket and Cricketers* (n.d. but probably 1890)

Nyren, John, *The Young Cricketer's Tutor* (first published in 1833, this edn. 1974)

Pearson, Harry, *The Trundlers,* (2013)

Peebles, Ian, *Spinner's Yarn* (1977)

Robertson-Glasgow, R.C. *Cricket Prints* (1943)
        More Cricket Prints (1948)
        46 Not Out (1948)

Robinson, Ray, *Between Wickets*

Snow, John, *Cricket Rebel* (1976)

Steel, A.G. and Lyttleton, R.H., *Cricket: Badminton Library* (1893)

Trueman, Freddie, *Ball of Fire: an Autobiography* (1976)

Warner, P.F., *The Book of Cricket* (1911)
        Cricket Between Two Wars (1942)

Winder, Robert, *The Little Wonder: The Remarkable History of Wisden* (2013)

Wynne-Thomas, Peter, *The History of Nottinghamshire CCC* (1992)